THE MANUAL

Weedon's Way

The Pain-Free Way: A Swing for Golfers with Bad Backs

by
Reeves Weedon
P.G.A. Advanced Fellow

Grosvenor House
Publishing Limited

All rights reserved
Copyright © Reeves Weedon, 2022

The right of Reeves Weedon to be identified as the author of this work has been asserted by him in accordance with Section 78 of the Copyright, Designs and Patents Act 1988

The book cover picture is copyright to Inmagine Corp LLC

This book is published by
Grosvenor House Publishing Ltd
28-30 High Street, Guildford, Surrey, GU1 3EL.
www.grosvenorhousepublishing.co.uk

This book is sold subject to the conditions that it shall not, by way of trade or otherwise, be lent, resold, hired out or otherwise circulated without the author's or publisher's prior consent in any form of binding or cover other than that in which it is published and without a similar condition including this condition being imposed on the subsequent purchaser.

A CIP record for this book
is available from the British Library

ISBN 978-1-80381-256-4
eBook ISBN 978-1-80381-305-9

Contents

Foreword: Dr J. Bryan Dixon vii

Preface: How it all started ix

Chapter 1: Introduction 1

Chapter 2: How to teach yourself (or others) Weedon's Way 6

Chapter 3: How Weedon's Way creates the seven phases 13

Chapter 4: Checkpoints 16

Chapter 5: Faults, fixes and drills 24

Chapter 6: Teaching 28

Chapter 7: Special situations 35

Chapter 8: Tailored teaching 40

Chapter 9: Case studies 46

Chapter 10: More advanced analysis 52

Chapter 11: How Weedon's Way differs from other approaches 69

Chapter 12: Injury prevention – to save your back 71

Chapter 13: Research 74

Foreword

Dr J. Bryan Dixon

1414 W. Fair Ave, Suite 190
Marquette, Michigan 49855
PHONE (906) 225-1321
(800) 462-6367
FAX (906) 228-9371
www.AdvancedOrthoandPlastics.com

To Whom It May Concern,

This letter is to serve as a recommendation and introduction of Reeves Weedon. Mr. Weedon is a PGA professional and research collaborator I have worked with since 2014. He has had a distinguished career in golf with a long track record of success in competition, instruction and business management within the sport and industry.

Mr. Weedon has spent his life studying, teaching and playing golf, becoming an expert in the biomechanics of the golf swing. His experience and inquiries led him to develop unique theories and teaching methods that challenge the current paradigm of golf instruction. In 2012 he published the book, *Phase 7 Swing: Powerful Ball-Striking Made Simple*. The books logical reasoning based on the principles of physics attracted the attention of scientists and clinicians who have worked with him to empirically investigate his claims.

In addition to his two published books, he has recently worked with a group of international researchers to produce two peer reviewed scientific research abstracts which have been presented at the American College of Sports Medicine, and a scientific paper currently under peer review. We expect an additional scientific paper to be submitted for peer reviewed publication by the end of the year. This is a breathtaking accomplishment and a line of investigation with real world applications including the reduction of lower back injuries in golf, extending the longevity and performance of current golfers and increasing the percentage of new golfers that stay within the sport.

Mr. Weedon's iconoclastic ideas and willingness to subject his theories to critical scientific appraisal make him a singular figure in the industry. His commitment to the rigorous and often tedious process of scientific research has placed him at the forefront of investigating not just the optimal biomechanics of the golf swing but also the pathomechanics of golf related injuries. His insights on the golf swing have become the basis of an ongoing international research project that has the potential to revolutionize golf performance, pedagogy and injury prevention.

I have full confidence that you will come to share our deep appreciation of his expertise, originality and collegiality as we continue ongoing research and clinical collaborations with him.

Sincerely,

J. Bryan Dixon, MD

Sports Medicine Physician and Partner, Advanced Center for Orthopedics and Plastic Surgery
Associate Clinical Professor, Michigan State University College of Human Medicine
Medical Director for Sports Medicine, UP Health Systems

Kenneth A. Davenport, MD ~ Wallace G. Pearson II, MD ~ Robert H. Blotter, MD ~ Jason D. Doppelt, MD ~ Nathan S. Taylor, MD ~ Zachary C. Leonard, MD Timothy B. Neuschwander, MD ~ J. Bryan Dixon, MD ~ Bradley Q. Warlick, MD ~ James W. Gallagher, DPM ~ Nathan J. Loewen, DPM

Preface

How it all started

It all started with *Newton on the tee*.

> *The golfer generates power through sequential movements of force through the larger muscle groups into the smaller muscles and an accelerated motion in order to gain the highest clubhead speed at the moment of impact.*
> —**Taras V. Kochno, M.D.,**
> **Sports Medicine and Rehabilitation International**

Because the "sequential movements of force", or mechanics, of a functional golf swing are rooted in the empirical world of physics, it is helpful for the average golfer to gain at least a cursory understanding of the observations of Sir Isaac Newton, a physicist whose laws of classical mechanics first explained motion in the 17th century, and any other scientific principles that significantly govern the swing. I know you didn't buy this book to master physics (you want to learn Weedon's Way), so our discussion will be brief and devoid of technical gobbledygook.

Thus, a tiny bite of Newton-Lite is all that is necessary to help with the mastery of the mechanics of the golf swing.

Understanding how the world of physics applies to the golf swing can not only provide the analytical tools to assess one's performance but also form a solid base for making any changes that might improve one's play.

So let's step up to the tee and find out what insights Sir Isaac Newton has contributed to our understanding of the golf swing. Of Newton's three laws of motion, one is especially important for the mastery of Weedon's Way. This Newtonian principle explains how we initiate the kinetic chain that launches those 300-metre drives. Although Newton's first and second laws apply also to the golf, swing we will not discuss them in any detail here.[1]

Newton on the tee

Sir Isaac Newton's three laws of motion form the basis for modern physics. His laws apply to golf. In a capsule, here's how.

Newton's first law of motion

Newton's first law says that an object in motion will remain in motion until it is acted upon by an outside force. We know that a golf ball moves when a force is applied to it. We also know that a golf ball always stops, even it is merely rolling down a fairway unimpeded. Therefore, it can be concluded that there are always outside forces acting on an object.

There are many outside forces acting on a golf ball that prevent it from moving in its original direction forever. Gravity pulls the ball towards the earth, preventing it from

---

[1] If you want to know more, you can find information about Newton laws on the internet at http://www.physicsclassroom.com/class/newtlaws.

travelling on the straight-line path it took when the club struck the ball. Air resistance, a form of friction, slows the ball's velocity as it travels through the air. Once a golf ball hits the ground again, friction is increased because a grassy or sandy surface creates much more friction with the ball than air.

Newton's second law of motion

Newton's second law of motion can be stated with this equation:

Force = Mass x Acceleration

Mass is the amount of matter an object has per unit of time that it is travelling. Force is the product of acceleration and mass. In simpler terms, if a really big thing is moving at you with that same acceleration, the big thing is going to hurt a heck of lot more because its force is much greater.

Newton's second law prevails throughout golf. When a golfer chooses a wood to hit off of the tee, he will probably choose the driver if he is looking for the greatest distance possible that he can achieve with his swing. The clubhead mass of the driver is greater than that of all other golf clubs. Even if he swings with the same club acceleration as with the other clubs, the driver should theoretically outdrive all other clubs because of the extra force that is imparted on the ball at the moment of impact with the club.

An alternative way to increase distance on a drive is by swinging faster. If a golfer swings faster than usual and meets the ball squarely, extra force will be created because the acceleration of the mass of the ball has been increased. Using the techniques of Weedon's Way you can swing faster by moving your body more quickly when pivoting. The increased speed of your rotation—that is, the pivot—feeds momentum down the shaft to the clubhead by way of conservation of angular momentum.

Accelerating the movement of the big muscles of the torso and upper body is a more consistent way to increase speed, and thus shot distance, because you keep the hands quiet through impact. The wrists square the clubface at impact without additional, conscious manipulation.

Newton's third law of motion

Newton's third law of motion states that for every reaction, there is an equal and opposite reaction. When a force is applied to the inside back of a golf ball with a club by swinging (the action), the ball rockets down the fairway (the reaction). If a golfer does not meet the ball squarely with his club, he produces a reaction that may be undesirable. A slice, where the ball fades off to the right for a right-handed player or to the left for a left-handed player, is caused by a golfer not meeting the ball squarely. In a slice, the golfer makes uneven contact with the ball, imparting a tight spin on the ball that is similar to that of a curveball thrown by a pitcher in baseball.

A hook is similar to the slice, except that the uneven contact results in the ball spinning in the opposite direction (to the right for a lefty, to the left for a righty). A hook acts in a similar manner as when a baseball hitter "pulls the ball", except that there is a much more vicious sidewards spin on the ball in a hook, taking it far off course from its original straight-line path to the target.

PREFACE

According to Newton's third law, for every action force there is an equal (in size) and opposite (in direction) reaction force. Forces always come in pairs—known as "action–reaction force pairs". Identifying and describing action–reaction force pairs is a simple matter of identifying the two interacting objects and making two statements describing *who is pushing on whom* and in what direction. For example, consider a baseball approaching the plate and colliding with the barrel of the batter's bat.

Now consider gravity and the downward pressure created by the muscles of the legs as the feet push into the turf while at address and during the golf swing. You create this pressure through the bending and straightening of the legs at the knees.

The turf or ground, aided by friction, pushes upwards. The pair of forces, pushing in opposite directions, cause the feet to remain firmly planted in the sod.

The golf swing begins with this firm foundation, the feet set shoulder width or slightly wider apart. The feet function much like the anchoring roots of a tree—the tree's roots keep it in place and the feet, when properly engaged, prevent lateral movement of the body. ***The bending and straightening of the legs at the knees create the rotary motion that keeps the body over the ball and prevents drifting.***

During the pivot of the golf swing the feet push down hard on the turf, allowing the hips to swivel or turn around the fixed axis of the spine. The ground pushes upwards, keeping the feet in place, the head over the ball and the torso centred between the feet.

The result of these powerful opposing forces is the formation of a rock-solid platform for the body's pivot.

The core of the body, which controls this pivot, harnesses the power of the body's mass as it turns around the spine. The magnitude of this power is raised by increasing the downward pressure of the feet and gravity because—as Newton's third law predicts— it produces an equal force pushing upwards.

The significant force needed to rotate the body's core is greatly assisted by a stable base. There is no wobble, no drift, no lateral slide. And the rotation of this large mass of the body takes place along what is known as the body's transverse plane, which is a plane that dissects the body along a plane that is perpendicular to the angle of the spine. Thus, when a player tilts his spine approximately 30 degrees at address—and maintains this spine angle throughout the swing—he makes the most powerful swing. All of this starts with the paired forces at work during address as described in Newton's third law.

This kinetic sequence requires dynamic balance to prevent a lateral leakage of the power and a stationary head to avoid moving the bottom of the swing rearward.

How to make a good pivot

In this chapter we've been learning about forming the platform for a good pivot, which begins with a solid and rooted address position. So, what exactly is a good pivot? First, the upper spine must be as straight as possible. For every degree that your spine rounds from the bottom of the shoulder blades to the back of the neck you lose 1½ degrees of rotation. This is a serious flaw, as Weedon's Way depends on a full and powerful pivot.

The spine at address needs to be set up at an angle that is 90 degrees or perpendicular to the shaft of the club.

The rotation of the shoulders also needs to be 90 degrees or perpendicular to the spine during the backswing and through the swing. This allows for a rotation along the transverse plane. The lower body must remain stable and support the coiling of the torso and rotation of the shoulders.

Do not focus on the shoulder turn. Instead, focus on bending and straightening the legs at the knees. When turning back or away from the ball, straighten the right leg and bend the left leg, the knee moving towards the target line and not towards the right knee (or back along a line parallel to the target line). When turning forward, straighten the left leg and bend the right knee, turning it to face the target as the weight is release to the left side at impact and beyond.

When turning the right hip around, back and away from the ball, be careful—some players turn too much. The result is that the knees do not work properly, causing the lower body to break down and lose balance. Players who turn too much forget that the body has to drive onto the front leg—which is straightening during the through swing and at impact— and unwind through the ball. *Video footage of an overturn in the backswing shows the club slowing down, not accelerating, at impact.* The acceleration of the clubhead must come from the lower body driving and the torso pivoting around the inside of the front leg to eliminate the swing flaw of solely turning the shoulders too far around the back in the backswing, because the clubhead goes directly up and allows the player to get behind the ball without any excessive raising of the club (above the right shoulder). Thus, the Weedon's Way swing virtually eliminates a problem before it can develop.

The next move is to exchange the body weight that is pressing down on the turf. Shift this weight from the rear heel to the front foot, rolling it onto the outside and, at the finish, to the toes. Unwind the upper body, bringing the arms and hands down alongside the body and firing the clubhead through the hitting zone.

Your entire body—but especially the legs and torso—controls the amount of the turn that takes place in the swing. It provides a certain amount of resistance that restricts the rotation of your hips and shoulders. If you should concentrate on turning any single part, that is the shoulders or the right hip, you risk getting out of synchronisation. Don't overly think about the pivot, except to focus on the pumping or flexing action of the knees. We should heed the advice of legendary teacher Harvey Penick: "The turn is a natural movement of the body . . . you will read and hear many complex instructions about the turn, but not from me."

What is conservation of angular momentum (COAM)?

Weedon's Way is a practical application of the science of physics, specifically the rotation around an axis, or angular momentum, whose principles or laws are partially expressed in what is called the conservation of angular momentum (COAM). This was first explained in print approximately 50 years ago by Joe Dante in his groundbreaking book, *Four Magic Moves to Winning Golf*. COAM is an integral part of Weedon's Way, so with Mr. Dante providing the steering wheel and the laws of physics providing the guardrails, let's take a ride down the COAM road and learn how COAM governs what we do when hitting a golf ball. And, most importantly, let's take a look at how COAM works in the Weedon's Way swing.

PREFACE

Physics tells us that when an object rotates around a fixed axis, it rotates at a constant rate of speed provided the object stays at the same distance from the axis. If the object is brought closer to the axis, it automatically speeds up; if it is moved farther out from the axis, it slows down.

Picture a spinning figure skater who moves his arms further away from his body to slow his speed, or closer to his body to increase his speed. Whichever way he positions his arms, the momentum itself is conserved. For example, with the skater's arms pinned to his chest, the momentum is distributed into the mass of his body. A corollary to this physical law is that the momentum will be distributed to the part of the system that has the lesser mass, or to the part that is easiest to move. This is an important principle when applied to the Weedon's Way swing; in fact, when applied to any properly executed swing.

So how does COAM apply?

Assume that the club and player make up the mechanical system and that the axis of rotation—clockwise in the backswing and counterclockwise in the downswing and follow-through—is the angled line created by the tilted spine. In the backswing, when the club is raised and the body pivots clockwise, the arms and club are positioned very close to the axis. When the rotational action is started on the downswing, the arms start down and away from the axis. As the arms and hands move away from the axis, they move very quickly on the way down (aided by gravity) and continue to accelerate as they pass by the front of the rear (right) leg. All of this is experienced in the downswing and the early transition to impact. However, as they approach impact, they begin to slow down (thanks to high-speed stop-action photography we can confirm this phenomenon).

However, the momentum is conserved and not lost. Rather than dissipating, it feeds directly into the shaft and clubhead, thus increasing the speed of the club as it enters the impact zone. In effect, the clubhead, now the recipient of the momentum, accelerates and catches up to the hands at impact, and passes them in the follow-through. The momentum of the hands—a player with strong arms and hands can generate more— contributes to the speed of the club, but not nearly as much speed as the law of COAM provides the clubhead. The result is speed and power at impact.

What happened? The Weedon's Way swing harnessed one of the laws governing physical matter. *The momentum was distributed to the part of the system with the lesser mass—the clubhead.*

Imagine a man cracking a bullwhip, whose tip when snapped can break the speed of sound. The momentum passes from the arm and hand and butt of the whip into the steadily tapering lash to the very light tip, which has the least mass. The same principle of COAM that snaps the bullwhip, resulting in a loud crack, also governs the golf swing.

By way of a marvel of nature, a stationary round ball no more than 4.3 centimetres in diameter and just slightly less than 46 grams in weight can rise and soar through the air the full length of a polo field—300 metres—and beyond when it collides with a speeding mass of 200 grams of titanium fixed at the bottom of a steel shaft.

From the research lab—Weedon's Way certified

Researchers continue to study the swing with sensors, Iron Byron, computers and video. We would be remiss if

PREFACE

we didn't consider what the camera captures, what the computers compute and what those who observe record. Here are a few nuggets about the secondary role of the arms, the importance of body rotation (the pivot), and a few other swing phenomena that reflect favourably on Weedon's Way principles.

1. Backswing: The arms do not start the backswing. The kinesic purpose of the backswing is to stretch the muscles that will propel the club.
2. Forward swing: The arms are taken along by the body, that is, the unwinding of the hips and the upper body (the forward pivot). Without trunk rotation, a loss of motion happens that enables the body segments to transmit maximum velocity to the clubhead at impact (loss of COAM). The body can generate as much as four horsepower (using the big muscles of the trunk and legs).
3. Pivot: Your hip muscles are the largest in the body and you must learn to use their potential power—hence Weedon's Way's emphasis on the centripetal and centrifugal force of the rotary swing. When the entire body is rotating, swinging the club takes less muscular effort.
4. Maximum COAM: When you move the clubhead as far away from the ball as possible, as many as 24 feet for a John Daly-like swing arc, you create the greatest potential for maximum acceleration of the clubhead through impact. Travelling at 100 mph, a driver head sends the ball away at about 135 mph. However, the hands are actually slowing down at impact, so a backswing that exceeds an optimum number of feet can—and will—result in less speed, diminished power and fewer metres of the tee.

Coefficient of restitution

Coefficient of restitution (COR) of two colliding objects is a fractional value representing the ratio of speeds after and before an impact. For two objects to register a COR of zero, the objects would "stop" at the collision, not bouncing at all.

The COR entered the golf world when golf club manufacturers began making thin-faced drivers with a so-called "trampoline effect" that creates drives of a greater distance as a result of an extra bounce off the clubface.

When the ball is struck by the club, it is deformed and flattened by the force of impact (balls with harder cores deform less than softer balls). The upper limit of COR permitted by golf's governing bodies is 0.83; golf balls typically have a COR of about 0.78.

The COR of the ball varies between different types of balls In general, a harder ball will travel further than a softer ball because it deforms less and will efficiently transfer more energy from club to ball. To obtain maximum distance in the drive, a ball must be selected that maximises restitution for the club speed. If the chosen ball is too soft for the club speed, too much energy will be spent deforming the ball and not enough energy will be stored in the ball. Similarly, if the ball is too hard for the club speed, then the ball will not deform enough and, again, will not transfer adequate energy. It is important to choose a ball that matches the club speed.

Centrifugal pulling action

Fellow teaching pro and Top 100 *Golf Magazine* Instructor David Glenz in his book, *Lowdown from the Lesson Tee*, offers some insight into the critical relationship between the pivot and the through swing, from the dropping of the club to initiate it to the point beyond impact. Glenz correctly debunks the misconception that "the left arm controls the swing".

I agree with Glenz's assertion that pulling down with your left arm, if strictly followed without assistance and some kind of coordination with the rest of the body, will shut down the centrifugal force that propels the clubhead. That's because the lower body initiates the swing. The arms never go first, and they never work alone.

If the left arm works alone at any time during the swing, that is, if it is not part of a sequence of motions, as this idea unfortunately suggests, you cannot build clubhead speed. And without clubhead speed you're left with no power to strike the ball.

Picture a baseball batter swinging at a pitch without the hips opening and the torso unwinding—this happens when an off-speed (slower) pitch fools the batter. This produces a weak swing, initiated and completed by the hands and arms only. Missing is the all-important pivot that I believe is the motor that drives the swing—in baseball and in golf.

Yes, the flailing batter's lead arm (the left arm for a right-handed batter) would gradually straighten just beyond the point of contact as would occur in a correctly executed swing. But without the lower-body platform that allows the batter to pivot, the bat would transmit very little energy to the ball. In fact, a Major League fastball at 95mph would likely knock the bat from the batter's hand. Everything is wrong with this picture. There is no speed of the barrelhead, minimal transfer of energy to the ball upon contact and absolutely no chance of knocking the ball beyond the infielders.

In the golf swing, you suffer similar consequences when you pull down or forward with the left arm without coordinating this with the coiling action of the leg, hips and torso. You need more than the arm pulling the head of the club forward or down. You need the big muscles of the legs and torso to turn the body and create the centrifugal speed that builds in the forward-moving clubhead. You need the uncoiling of the back and side muscles of the torso to create this centrifugal pulling action. The arms, hands and clubhead are propelled to high speed by centrifugal force. When applied to the ball with a clubface that is squared as well as following the target line, the ball will fly straight and true.

Newcomers to golf who were former athletes, dancers, martial arts practitioners—those who have learned how to control their body in athletic movement—more easily learn Weedon's Way because their physical platform for delivering the clubhead is more stable than that of the average student. If you can control your body and maintain superior balance, you can master golf by the Weedon's Way method faster than any other method.

Chapter 1

Introduction

a. A simple instruction (flex the left knee down and up)
   1. First golf lesson should be without a club (leg drill)
b. Why it works.
   1. Flow of energy coordinates
   2. Power creates shape
   3. The ground powers the swing
   4. The legs create the rotation
   5. Gravity must be able to work on the club
   6. Pushing mass in the ground creates momentum
   7. The hardest action in golf is to move the club; once it is going it will move itself: just hang on for the ride!
c. Ground reaction forces
d. Injury prevention

Weedon's Way is easy to describe and quick to learn, but behind this simplicity lies basic physics and physiology, and years of study and experience. The swing can be learned in minutes, but, as with most forms of human performance, it takes practice to maximise its full expression. And, also as with other forms of human performance, it is vitally important to get the few critical movements exactly right from the start.

When we see a golf swing, the eye is drawn to the dramatic movements of the golf club, therefore we naturally assume that the way to produce the swing is to heave the club around with the arms and shoulders. In reality, however, the power to move the club comes from the ground.

All instructions and descriptions in this manual are for right-handed golfers. If you are left-handed, please reverse them.

a. A simple instruction (flex the left knee down and up)

To produce Weedon's Way, address a golf ball with a golf club, then flex the left knee and extend the right knee. Allow this lower body action to move the rest of the body, which should turn slightly to the right. The body weight will be to the left. Then reverse the knees: flex the right knee and extend the left knee quickly. This action will rotate the upper body to the left and provide an inertial impulse to accelerate the golf club towards the ball. The feel of the swing is more down and up than right and left. It is a swing, an athletic, dynamic movement.

1. First golf lesson should be without a club (leg drill)

The best way to familiarise yourself with the feeling of Weedon's Way is to do the exercise called the "leg drill". Stand facing another golfer and hold hands, both with knees and hips slightly flexed. Both now flex the left knee and extend the right knee, rotating the upper body to the right. Then reverse the knees, flexing the right knee and extending the left knee, rotating the upper body to the left. These actions will cause each person's arms to pull on their partner's arms. This should be the first lesson for a new lower body golfer.

b. Why it works

Weedon's Way works because pushing on the ground with the powerful leg and hip muscles causes rapid rotation of the upper body.

1. *Flow of energy coordinates*

Scientists say, "The flow of energy through a system serves to organise that system."[2] The act of pushing on the ground provides the energy that flows through the body and coordinates the correct sequence of movements to maximally accelerate the club towards the ball. The golfer is not required to master, or attend to, the myriad small movements that are required by other golf swings.

2. *Power creates shape*

The most difficult action in golf is to move the club. This is why golfers often take a long time to get their swing started. Unlike other approaches, in Weedon's Way the golfer doesn't move the club; instead, they move their legs. The club is

---

[2] Harold J. Morowitz, *Energy Flow in Biology* (New York/London: Academic Press, 1968).

moved passively. Once the club starts moving it will move itself; the golfer just hangs on.

3. The ground powers the swing

In Weedon's Way, the legs cause body rotation. Our measurements show that twice as much rotational momentum can be created in this way as in the conventional golf swing (see chapter 10).

4. The legs create the rotation

In Weedon's Way, pushing on the ground with the legs provides the necessary power.

5. Gravity must be able to work on the club

The power that is provided by pushing the legs on the ground creates the shape of the swing, and ultimately the shape of the ball flight. Control of the shape of the ball flight is gained through power. In other words, the harder the ball is hit, the more control the golfer has over its trajectory.

6. Pushing mass into the ground creates momentum

The more the golfer pushes into the ground, the more power and control are gained. As with athletic moves in other sports, the more the golfer pushes their mass into the ground, the more momentum is created.

7. The hardest action in golf is to move the club; once it is going it will move itself: just hang on for the ride!

Because the lower body is doing the job of creating power, rotation and inertial impulse, the upper body is allowed to react to these forces. Importantly, because the upper body is not moving the club, gravity is allowed to act. This adds acceleration and shape to the swing, unlike conventional swings that require the club to be manipulated into the correct position.

c. Ground reaction forces

As we have mentioned, according to Newton's third law, for every action force there is an equal (in size) and opposite (in direction) reaction force. Forces always come in pairs, known as "action–reaction force pairs." Describing action–reaction force pairs is a simple matter of identifying the two interacting objects: in Weedon's Way these are the pumping legs and the ground.

d. Injury prevention

The axis tilt, which is a sliding of the hips at the start of the downswing, starts the kinetic chain in the upper body (modern) golf swing. This bumping hip movement towards the target also shallows the shaft, regains loft on the clubface and creates a connection with the ground pre-impact. This motion, which is a must for the classic swing, puts too much torque on the spine and is a significant cause of lower back pain and injury in the golf swing.

Weedon's Way has no axis tilt, therefore creates little or no torque on the spine and helps to prevent lower back injury.

An axis tilt in the golf swing is, in my opinion, like giving arsenic for a bellyache!

Chapter 2

How to teach yourself (or others) Weedon's Way

a. What is PPFPP?
   1. Unconditional positive regard
   2. Always first principles
   3. A few relentless principles
   4. Access new sensory modalities
   5. Iconoclasm
   6. New performance standards
   7. Either easy or impossible
   8. The subject will tell you when they get the hook
   9. Need to use alternative descriptors

b. Useful images and phrases

c. Pay attention to sound

d. Look for high flight

e. Transverse body pivot (front to back/back to front, feels down to up, and very left sided)

f. Left arm under right shoulder

g. The arms are dead/value the club's weight

Teaching Weedon's Way, to yourself or to another golfer, is similar to coaching other forms of human performance, with perhaps one significant difference. That difference involves the necessity of convincing the student, particularly if that student has received previous golfing tuition, to trust that the ground will power the swing. No "help" from the arms, hands or shoulders is useful. Unlike the conventional swing, you do not need to try to turn your hips or shoulders: the force flowing through your body will look after these matters, if you allow them to.

Most golfing instruction teaches students about specific locations that the club and parts of the body are supposed to occupy at various stages of the swing. In Weedon's Way, there are no positions. The flow of energy, if unimpeded, coordinates the correct phasing of movements. (For evidence, see chapter 10c.)

a. What is PPFPP?

Having observed successful coaching sessions with golfers of varying levels of experience and ability, we have identified characteristics of interactions that are important to attend to. We call this attention "Psychological Priming for Physical Performance" (PPFPP). These are the principles of PPFPP:

1. Unconditional positive regard

The coach must have unconditional positive regard for the student, especially if it is yourself. All comments and suggestions must be made in a positive light. Golf is played with a long lever arm, and the resultant leverage amplifies mistakes and can result in feelings of negativity. Positive regard and affirming comments build positive attitudes.

2. Always first principles

Because learners are seldom familiar with using ground forces, the coach needs to focus relentlessly on the basic elements of Weedon's Way. The energy from the ground will coordinate the body correctly. It is counter-productive to attend to the finer points such as grip, body positions or timing until later.

3. A few relentless principles

The coach needs to be in the learner's head with phrases that will help the learner to concentrate on using the ground. This requires constant emphasis on the coordinating principles of Weedon's Way, particularly the transverse pivot.

4. Access new sensory modalities

It is helpful for learners to call to their attention sensory feedback they might otherwise ignore. Two examples are the sound of a well-struck shot and the height of a well-struck shot.

5. Iconoclasm

Most golfers bring with them an idea about how to achieve a golf swing. Learning Weedon's Way usually requires forgetting this conventional—or even just incorrect—information. For example, a beginner typically has erroneous ideas about the speed of the backswing and the downswing (the ground forces take care of these). The coach can assist the transition to the new swing by sustaining an iconoclastic attitude.

6. *New performance standards*

It is helpful for learners to call to their attention aspects of their performance they might otherwise ignore. Two examples are the distance of a shot and the shape of the trajectory (the draw). And the ball never starts to the left of its intended target.

7. *Either easy or impossible*

There is nothing difficult about Weedon's Way. When the legs are moved correctly and the rest of the body is allowed to react, the ball will go up into the air and fly in a proper trajectory. The learner needs regular encouragement that it is easy and that they will be able to do it. The advantages of using Weedon's Way are instantly visible. You just need to get out of the way of yourself and hang on to the Big Mo!

8. *The subject will tell you when they get the hook*

If the coach is paying attention, the student will unambiguously communicate to the coach which teaching approach was successful. The learner will tell the coach when they "get the hook", but the telling will not be verbal. Coach and learner need to remain in constant communication, and the coach just has to tap into the learner's "lingo".

9. *Need to use alternative descriptors*

It usually takes several different approaches to communicate a change to a learner. The coach must try multiple metaphors and incorporate multiple images. Often the simplest formulations work best – for example, "big legs" is a better cue than "scientific studies show that flexing your left knee to 120 degrees is optimum."

b. Useful images and phrases

Certain phrases seem to be especially helpful in teaching Weedon's Way. It is helpful if these phrases are repeated quietly while the golfer is beginning the swing. The effect is to replace the golfer's unhelpful swing thoughts with more productive ones. Here are some examples:

- "Come out of golf." As long as the golfer is attempting to match their movements to an idealised set of movements, they will interfere with the flow of energy. This phrase encourages the golfer to try something new.
- "Let it go." This is another way of encouraging the golfer to allow the ground forces to move their body. This applies as much on the backswing as on the downswing.
- "The arms are dead." This means not engaging the muscles of the arms and shoulders.
- "Heavy arms." This also means not engaging arm and shoulder muscles.
- "What's heavy going up is light coming down." Most poor golfers reverse this, snatching the club upwards and fighting to move it down fast.
- "Value the weight of the club." This is an alternative sensory modality to call to the learner's attention. Many poor golfers are oblivious to the weight of the club, particularly with longer clubs.

- "Let gravity work on the club." If the arms are passive and if the club is heavy going up, then gravity will act on the club, adding acceleration and allowing the club to fall into the position that creates "lag", the timing that maximises power.
- "Poor players are in a hurry to get down; good players want never to get there." Time at the top allows gravity to work on the club and power from the legs to coordinate the body.
- "Go down and up." Weedon's Way feels very vertical. It is necessary to come up in order to clear space for the club.
- "When the shaft and the neck meet, the swing is complete." Learners need to embrace the momentum created by the ground.
- "The ball is your target." Learners frequently worry about a distant target such as a green and ignore the ball. All golfers have this problem when they move from practice tee to the course.

c. Pay attention to sound

Weedon's Way delivers the club to the ball with maximum force and square alignment. One result is the loud "pop" of a properly struck ball. A loud noise is an indicator of a correctly executed swing.

d. Look for high flight

Weedon's Way maintains loft on the club through the swing. Consequently, the ball flight will be high. High flight adds distance and control, and is an indicator of a correctly executed swing.

e. Transverse body pivot

The core of Weedon's Way is the transverse pivot. If the legs are moved in the correct way and the upper body remains passive, then the weight will move from front to back and then from back to front. The feeling is of going down and up and is very left sided.

f. Left arm under right shoulder

In Weedon's Way there is no axis tilt. (This refers to a feature of the conventional swing that requires the body to kink sidewards towards the right hand to avoid the club hitting the right shoulder.) Because the left arm is below the right shoulder, gravity is allowed to work on the club so that it can fall without hitting the right shoulder. An aligned axis helps to prevent back injuries and maintains loft on the clubface.

g. The arms are dead/value the club's weight

When the legs drive the transverse pivot and the upper body remains passive, the angle assumed by the body at address will cause the club to rise. The arms do not raise the club. At the top of the backswing the left arm is across the chest, and it does not rise above the right shoulder. The club is necessarily in a position of "heavy lag". This means it is the final element in a chain of moving parts. This allows gravity to act on the club and increase power.

Chapter 3

How Weedon's Way creates the seven phases

a. Phase, not position.

b. Allow the ground to cause them to happen.

a. Phase, not position

In my book, *The Phase Seven Golf Swing*,[3] I set out the basics of Weedon's Way. As the title suggests, the book focuses on the phases through which the club passes during the swing. In physics, "phase" is a comparison of the relative position of two things. In the book I describe the relative positions of the clubhead to the body.

We have sought the clues that would correctly put golfers through the phases. Over time we have come to see that concentrating on the production of ground force coupled with

---

[3] Reeves Weedon, *The Phase Seven Golf Swing* (Pennington: Mountain Lion, 2012).

proper use of the large leg and hip muscles, the phases happen by themselves.

b. Allow the ground to cause them to happen

Please understand that "phases" are not "positions". Each phase is a section of a sequence of continuous movement. It will not work to "put" the club in certain places because the swing is dynamic, like a line of falling dominoes: all that is needed is a starting impulse. The seven phases are descriptive, not proscriptive. This means that the golfer does not seek to learn, practise or master these phases (as do golfers practising the kinetic sequence in the conventional swing), but rather to allow the ground reaction force to move their body and club.

The physics underlying Weedon's Way is described in chapter 10, but it is worth stating here that Weedon's Way makes three physics-based improvements on the conventional swing. First, it maximises the conservation of angular momentum by not dissipating it in lateral moves. Second, it keeps the moment of inertia low (so the ground force can generate maximum clubhead speed) by keeping the body collected together and the club close. Third, Weedon's Way creates an inertial impulse that reroutes the club at the top of the backswing so that no energy-wasting "transition" move is required.

The power produced by the legs will naturally take the player through the phases, as long as there is no tampering with body and club movements. The power creates the shape of body and club movements, and it creates the shape of the ball flight. Nonetheless, understanding the phases is useful for coaches and learners to grasp how the ground moves the body and the club during Weedon's Way, and to have a language to discuss how to improve the swing.

The following chapter contains pictorial descriptions of the phase seven swing (Weedon's Way).

Chapter 4

Checkpoints

a. Left knee over left foot

b. Left arm over chest

c. Right leg straight

d. Weight left

e. Both legs jump

f. Ball is the target

g. Ball position

h. No axis tilt

i. Left knee/right knee/hip and shoulder

j. Left arm under right shoulder

k. Resist the throw-out/access gravity

l. Loft on the clubface

m. Arms have the same characteristics as the body

a. Left knee over left foot

b. Left arm over chest

c. Right leg straight

d. Weight left

e. Both legs jump

f. Ball is the target

g. Ball position

h. No axis tilt

i. Left knee/right knee/hip and shoulder

j. Left arm under right shoulder

k. Resist the throw-out/access gravity

l. Loft on the clubface

m. Arms have the same characteristics as the body

Chapter 5

Faults, fixes and drills

a. Arms lift

b. Not valuing weight of club

c. Missing the ball

d/e. Topping the ball/Thinning the ball

f. Slicing

g. Hooking

h. Needing more distance

Weedon's Way makes maximum use of the laws of physics and facts of human physiology. It is easy to learn and straightforward to teach. However, as with other forms of human performance, attaining skill takes practice. And, as with other forms of human performance, getting started correctly with the (few) basics can help to prevent many later problems. The trained eye of a coach or professional can also help to prevent problems by monitoring the learner's thoughts and movements as their skills develop.

Golf is a demanding game, and all players need to reconnect with the basics in order to be successful, so regular lessons are to be recommended. In golf there are many common pitfalls. Returning to the basics—the transverse pivot, club no higher than right shoulder, and big legs—fixes most problems. With reference to these few basics, here are some examples of particular swing flaws and ways to fix them.

a. Arms lift

Cause: arms swinging away from the body as the first move. Also the arms moving away from the body centre.

Fix: flexing left knee/extending right knee starts the golf swing (and the process of pushing into the ground). The arms then move in the direction of the body.

b. Not valuing weight of club

Causes: the arms initiate backswing lift which creates lack of momentum. Alternatively, the arms accelerate towards the ball on the downswing, which decreases loft and misses the centre of the strike.

Fix: using the ground. The legs power the backswing; the arms do nothing and are moved by body motion. Also, the inertial impulse of the legs pushing on the ground throws the club into the ball, without additional arm action. It is important to retain soft, free wrists.

c. Missing the ball

Causes: forgetting that the ball is your target; having only peripheral (or no) vision of the ball; acceleration or deceleration by the arms; weight shift not caused by the transverse pivot; shortening the lever arm by bending the elbows.

Fixes: first teach the learner to swing and miss the ball intentionally; use the drills that teach that what is heavy going up is light going down; help the golfer to feel gravity working on the downswing; make sure the ball is in the golfer's central vision. Repetition!

d/e. Topping the ball/Thinning the ball

Causes: lever shortening caused by shoulder tilting not related to the transverse pivot; tight wrists; acceleration or deceleration not caused by the transverse pivot; having only peripheral (or no) vision of the ball.

Fixes: the transverse pivot; soft, free wrists; drills that teach that what is heavy going up is light coming down; left arm remains below right shoulder; allowing gravity to work on the club.

f. Slicing

Causes: arms lifting; weight shifting laterally; acceleration from the top unrelated to legs pushing on the ground ("casting"); tightness in grip, wrists, hands or shoulders; set-up to ball wrong (ball too far forward; body aimed incorrectly); grip too weak.

Fixes: the transverse pivot; accessing gravity; using the ground; relaxed upper body; ensuring that arm movement has same characteristics as body movement; left arm under right shoulder; ball position near middle of stance.

g. Hooking

Causes: set-up issues, such as standing too far away from the ball; shoulders and hips aimed to the right; grip too strong; weight shift too right-sided in the downswing; body slowing at impact while club maintains maximum speed; grip too loose.

Fixes: transverse pivot; using the ground; ensuring that arm movement has same characteristics as body movement; left arm under right shoulder; accessing gravity.

h. Needing more distance

Causes: not accessing the ground; blocking the acceleration caused by the transverse pivot; moving everything too slowly.

Fix: allowing the legs to turn the lower body on the backswing and the inertial impulse produced by the legs to power the downswing.

Chapter 6

Teaching

a. Challenges
   1. Attitude
   2. Talent
   3. Focus

b. Groups

c. It doesn't look normal!

a. Challenges

When it comes to learning Weedon's Way, many players think they know enough about the golf swing in general but may not know how to learn it. They get caught up in truths that have always let them down and become confused with the simplicity of our coaching methods. My answer to this problem is always, "Get out of golf!"

Once you stop thinking "golf swing", Weedon's Way is very simple and achievable. Golf is an illogical game played by logical people. I say constantly to my students, "If it makes sense, don't believe it!"

The way people learn is based on the information given, and everyone does it a little differently. Some just want to think about their motion; others want to feel it, see it or just do it!

So the coach must always listen to what the learner is saying, as they always say what they want to be taught. Weedon's Way coach uses their ears more than their mouths.

The moral of our learning is the well-known acronym KISS – Keep It Simple, Stupid. If you come out of golf you will experience a unique kinaesthetic feel that will stripe it every time!

1. Attitude

Although it is widely known that there are four types of learners—people who do, people who feel, people who see and people who think—in my experience there are only two: people who want and people who don't want. Those who want, I call "students of the game"—they want to achieve their best golf. The don't wants I call "rodeo ponies"—you might as well enjoy the ride before they buck you off!

The students are people with little or no opinion of how the swing works. They will follow your instructions verbatim and be patient with their improvement. Other students in this category are those who have tried every method to no avail and are almost ready to give up, but don't want to. I find such people to be good learners because their past opinions have disappeared as a result of multiple failures. They cling to the rapid success of Weedon's Way and improve like never before.

Rodeo ponies spend more time telling you about what they are doing than listening to what they need to do. They are so caught up in technique that they are oblivious to the instruction, "Come out of golf!" They are, as we have said, logical people playing an illogical game. Rodeo ponies will book sessions with Weedon's Way coaches through recommendations from their friends who are playing unbelievably well. However, these students are not prepared to make changes like their friends have. The old adage comes to mind: "If you change nothing, nothing changes." And the rodeos refuse to change because they cannot understand the simplicity of coming out of golf in order to change their future. It reminds me of Einstein's definition of madness: people repeating the same thing, expecting change.

Having the right attitude is crucial to being a good learner.

2. *Talent*

Another word for talent, in my opinion, is "recovery". People who recover their swing the most are those their peers refer to as talented. Talent is not as important to learning Weedon's Way as attitude and focus. Talent will increase the purpose if the pupil is focused on the change in hand and has a good attitude. As a rule of thumb, if people are skilled at a particular game, they tend to play it more. Without practice and repetition they will not achieve the heights of success of which they are capable. A good attitude and focus are paramount to learning Weedon's Way. Talent is an optional extra.

3. *Focus*

When people choose golf as their main sporting activity, most assume they will be able to play a decent game. But often this is not the case, and in many cases year after year they do not attain the standard they wish for. Millions of golfers have devoted enough time and effort to their game to have attained a high standard if they had focused more on the correct things.

It pays to focus more on the ground that powers the swing. The legs that flex and extend against the ground push power into the body to coordinate the internal flow of energy. In Weedon's Way, we believe that if you focus on the physical power created by the body's relationship with the ground, it will recruit the correct muscles to enable you to hit the ball like an elite player. Focus is important. Focus on what is correct to science, not to the latest teaching fad.

b. Groups

It is simple to teach Weedon's Way to groups. Through ground-force dynamics, we believe that all students will be able to improve ball flight and increase distance. Group tuition is greatly assisted by use of two lower body drills.

The first of these is called the beginner's drill (leg drill). This introduces all golfers to the power of the ground on which we stand. Pushing in and against the ground creates power that the ordinary golfer will rarely have experienced. Here's how it goes.

Without a club, assume the address position, with arms hanging freely in front of the body. Then start pumping the legs, flexing the left leg at the knee and straightening the right leg simultaneously in order to rotate the core. This leg motion masters the rotary swing around a fixed axis (the spine). Be sure to keep your head steady. Continue to flex and extend the legs alternately, pushing into and off the ground until you build a good rhythm. Practise this drill for about five minutes every day, and you will develop a strong pivot to power the swing.

The other drill is called the flamingo drill. The name gives the task away. Stand on your left leg and raise your right leg in the air. Take a club in your right hand and pivot clockwise until your right shoulder and hip are behind you. Pause momentarily and then pivot anticlockwise to initiate striking a ball. Keep doing this until you feel your muscles ache. This drill will give you the feeling of a centred pivot, and will provide depth in the swing that will enhance its power. As with the beginner's drill, five minutes a day will create a muscle memory that will power the swing like never before.

It is simple to teach Weedon's Way to large groups of golfers, and they will make rapid improvement. Using golf drills is a must in group coaching.

c. It doesn't look normal!

Dick Fosbury used the "Fosbury Flop", a then unorthodox head-first back-to-the-bar method of high jumping, at the Mexico City Olympic Games in 1968. He cleared 2.24 metres to secure a gold medal and a world record. His method was later identified scientifically to be superior because it keeps the centre of the body mass below the bar. Before Fosbury, every high jumper went over the bar on their belly; after Fosbury, every high jumper did it his way.

A similar paradigm shift is now happening in the more popular game of golf because Weedon's Way is pure to scientific truths:

- The ground powers the swing.
- The moment of inertia is small.

TEACHING

- The mass to hit the ball is greater.
- Gravity can access the club.
- It abides by the law of conservation of angular momentum and Newton's three laws of force and motion.

So we took a big pot, put in all the above scientific components and mixed it up, not knowing quite what it would look like. It came out looking like the Weedon's Way golf swing, and it is pure and correct.

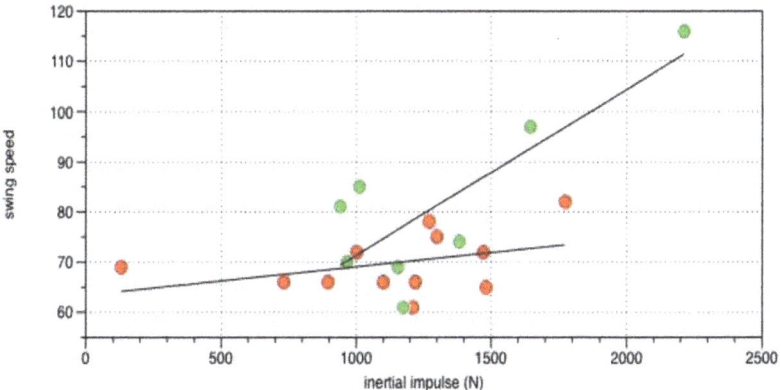

This graph charts the swing speeds of scratch golfers (green) and handicap golfers (red) against the total inertial impulse (force exerted on the ground from the top of the backswing till impact). The two linear regression lines show that for the same impulse a scratch golfer has higher swing speed. For example, the linear regression lines show that at 1500 N inertial impulse, a handicap golfer would be expected to have 72mph swing speed and a scratch golfer 88mph swing speed. This is an improvement of approximately 20 per cent (or more than 30 metres for a seven-iron hit 160 metres).

This difference in converting inertial impulse into swing speed is caused by faulty mechanics in the handicap golfer – typically, involving extraneous upper body motions. So what the coach is doing in Weedon's Way is getting the student to climb on to the steeper regression line!

Chapter 7

Special situations

a. Uphill lie

b. Downhill lie

c. Ball above your feet

d. Ball below your feet

e. High flight shot

f. Lower flight shot

g. Draw the ball

h. Fade the ball

i. Chipping (a short shot)

j. Pitching (longer and higher than a chip)

These are commonly known as awkward lies or speciality shots. Adjustments are usually made before the shot takes place so that the swing's environment is as normal. These shots are important to all golfers as they are the epoxy (glue) to every golfer's round.

a. Uphill lie

- Weight on the lower foot, so the body is perpendicular to the slope.
- Position the ball closer to the higher foot.
- Aim the blade and body to the right of your intended target.
- Swing as normal and the ball should fly right to left.
- For the uphill lie, always select more club as the height you will attain off the slope will mean loss of distance.

b. Downhill lie

- Weight on the lower foot, so the body is perpendicular to the slope.
- Position the ball nearer to the higher foot.
- Aim the blade and body to the left of the intended target.
- Swing as normal and the ball should fly left to right.
- Select less club as the slope will deloft the club and the ball will fly lower and further.

c. Ball above your feet

- Stand closer to the ball and grip the club slightly lower than usual.

SPECIAL SITUATIONS

- Weight should be evenly balanced.
- Ball should be positioned in the middle of the stance.
- Aim blade and body to the right of the target.
- Swing as normal and you should hit a right-to-left shot.

d. Ball below your feet

- Lower your centre of gravity at address by flexing your knees more. Retain this knee flex throughout the swing.
- Weight should be evenly balanced.
- Ball should be positioned left of centre.
- Aim blade and body to the left of the target.
- Swing as normal, retaining more flex in the knees, and you should hit a left-to-right-shot.

e. High flight shot

This shot is simple to achieve with Weedon's Way:

- Grip higher than usual on the club.
- Use more wrists.
- Grip pressure will be less (softer).
- Use the ground more. By doing this you will gain more length, along with a centred strike.

f. Lower flight shot

To produce a lower flight shot the principle is also simple. The task is to turn your two-lever system swing into one. It will resemble a long chip shot swing and will keep the ball flight down. To create a one-lever, tighten the wrist joint to make the arm and club work as a single unit from shoulder to clubhead.

- Grip the club lower to shorten the leverage.
- Tighten grip pressure and freeze the wrists.
- Use the ground less. By doing this you will also lose distance.

g. Draw the ball

The draw shot is produced before the shot is made, in the address. Simply move the ball back in your stance towards your back foot (for the right-handed player) and towards the toe on the clubface. Then swing as normal and enjoy the fruit of a soft draw.

h. Fade the ball

As with the draw, the fade is produced pre-shot. The ball is moved towards the player's front foot and towards the heel of the club. When swinging normally, a soft fade will appear.

Note: Do not accelerate at the ball with this shot. A better result will be attained by slowing down at impact.

i. Chipping (a short shot)

A chip shot is a one-lever movement. As in the low shot, simply freeze the wrist joint to make the arms and club move as one from shoulder to clubhead.

- Weight as normal. You may favour the front foot.
- Feet should be closer together than for a normal shot.

- Ball position middle/back.
- Aim as normal.
- Stand closer to the ball.
- Swing. As in a full swing, the legs power the chip shot by flexing and extending against the ground, although not as much, as less power is needed. The club doesn't go above the hips.

j. Pitching (longer and higher than a chip)

This uses the same technique as the chip shot but with the two-lever model. Defrost the wrists. The club swings higher than the hips, but not as high as in a full shot.

Chapter 8

Tailored teaching

a. Common challenges

   1. Rigidity
   2. Floppy looseness
   3. Physical limitations
   4. Lack of athletic experience

b. Beginners

c. Women

d. Children

e. The elderly

f. Those with disabilities

The future of golf depends on including all people. Golf offers terrific exercise, along with opportunities for social interaction, competition and kinaesthetic pleasure. But there are significant barriers to entry for much of the population. The biggest barrier may be the perception that golf is difficult to learn and that it takes a long time to become competent.

Weedon's Way offers the possibility of reducing the barriers to competency for populations who do not currently play golf. Experience shows that in the first lesson, a student using Weedon's Way—be they an adult, a child or a senior—can strike the ball solidly and get it up in the air. After a few lessons, and some practice, a student can become competent enough to play most courses.

At present, golf is dominated by men of working age, women of working age (who often face serious discrimination with regard to access to facilities and instruction) and retired people who learned to play when they were younger. There are golf programmes for juniors, but these are usually filled with the children of adult golfers. In this section we will consider how to use Weedon's Way to coach populations that are currently under-represented.

There are general principles that apply to working with all these populations, even though, of course, specific details need to be devised for each person. These are general principles that apply to teaching any new activity, particularly if the activity requires observed performance.

First, the student needs to feel that they are successful and don't appear foolish. Second, the student needs a conceptual framework and the physical experience of the feel of the ground force. All of the coaching techniques discussed in chapter 1 of this manual need to be ramped up, and the most important of these is a consistent positive attitude and message from the coach.

a. Common challenges

Here are some of the common challenges and fixes when tailoring coaching to the learner:

1. *Rigidity*

Causes: trying too hard; fear of failure; physical limitations; achievement orientation.

Fixes: lightness; celebrating successes; simple movements.

2. *Floppy looseness*

Causes: lack of athletic experience; no feeling for source of power.

Fixes: feeling the ground forces.

3. *Physical limitations*

Causes: many, including muscular/skeletal disorders, arthritis, eyesight, trauma.

Fixes: honest discussion; then accommodation to the movements of the transverse pivot.

4. *Lack of athletic experience*

Causes: lack of opportunity; fear.

Fixes: patience; focus on fundamentals.

b. Beginners

To most beginning adults, the golf swing is non-intuitive. The golf grip seems contrived. Turning your back to the target sounds like lunacy. As it is usually presented, the golf swing consists of thousands of moving parts that all require perfect timing. And it seems obvious that the only way to hit the ball far is to swing the club as fast as possible.

Weedon's Way massively reduces the chaos. Details that are usually focused on in conventional lessons—such as grip, stance, wrist cock, straight left arm—can all be ignored until much later. Once the student feels the club being moved by the inertial impulse generated through simple leg motions, they will be on the path to continued improvement.

The student is likely to expect either to perform like a professional or to fail utterly (perhaps as they have done in the past), so the coach needs to celebrate more prosaic milestones, such as the first ball struck, the first ball in the air, the first draw shape. The coach needs to counsel patience and repetition, and to be constantly feeding the student useful swing thoughts.

c. Women

Women beginners take well to Weedon's Way since, statistically, most of their strength is in the lower body and they have less experience than men at flailing at things with their arms. It remains critically important, however, that women feel the power that flows through their body from the ground forces and that they allow that power to shape and time their swings.

Women who have played some golf will face the same challenges as men do in letting go of ingrained swing thoughts and habits.

d. Children

Children need short, intense lessons and lots of praise. Young children often have a vast range of movement and can be slow to channel movements to the essential. It takes real care to enable a small child to feel the flow of power from the ground force couples. Playing with bigger, foam balls should be explored.

Older children benefit from repetition, which can be elicited with games and challenges.

e. The elderly

When teaching Weedon's Way to a senior, it is important to recognise that as the body ages, there is a gradual loss of strength along with a reduction in flexibility as deterioration of the muscular system reduces movement and speed. This will lead to the senior losing distance through the green. The transverse body pivoting against the ground through flexion and extension of the legs will regain the power in the swing that is lost as a result of ageing. Weedon's Way is a must for all seniors who want to prolong their golfing career.

f. Those with disabilities

When we speak of handicaps in golf, we immediately identify a player's ability through a number (a 24 or 6 handicap, for example). But there are golfers who play with other handicaps: those who are disabled. Whether the game is played by someone with a physical or a mental disability, golf should be a game that all can enjoy and reach a proficient standard.

The coach is probably more important in determining the success of the lesson programme for a learner with a disability than for any other learner. While all individuals, when being coached, must provide their own motivation, enthusiasm and patience, the coach can be supportive and sustain additional motivation and encouragement for those who face additional challenges.

The Weedon's Way coach, with their special teaching tools, can enable the learner to add power to the swing through wrists, legs or body during the teaching sessions.

Chapter 9

Case studies

a. Beginner

b. High handicapper

c. Low handicapper

d. Scratch player

e. Player with disabilities

a. Beginner

When working with a person who has never made a golf swing before, the first step would be an introduction to the ground we stand on. The ground provides the power to the swing, so the first thing to teach would be the beginner's leg drill.

This drill calls for an emphasis on a pumping action, or flexing of the left leg at the knee and rotation at the core. This is how the motion is produced: flex the left knee out towards the target line on which the ball sits. Extend the right leg as much as possible. Next, turn the right shoulder in or around to the back, away from the target line in a clockwise motion. When the right shoulder is turned approximately 90 degrees, the leg action can keep moving to push as much body mass into the ground as possible. Your core legs and shoulders have created muscular tension. Your feet are pressing into the ground, creating more force that will be released when the legs start pushing against the ground.

This alternate flexion and extension of the legs must be taken to the practice tee after the coaching session has finished. This drill will give the golf shot effortless power.

Once we have repeated this drill several times, the learner is given a golf club and asked on the backswing, after holding the club and addressing the ball, to flex the left leg and extend the right leg. Then on the downswing, to extend the left leg and flex the right leg. This takes place while allowing gravity to access the club and making a motion with the club at the ball.

The simplicity of this movement always gives flight to the ball in a beginner's first golf lesson. The layperson can understand and coordinate their weight, pressing down into the ground on the backswing as the club goes up. And as the weight is pushed up from the ground on the downswing, the club is thrown down at the ball.

The beginner's drill is essential for all learner golfers.

b. High handicapper

As with the beginner, we would hypothesise that this player's connection with the ground is poor as a result of their handicap. If this is the case, we would ask them to learn and practise the beginner's leg drill. Once the learner has mastered this drill sufficiently, loft on the clubface is a must to fit with the new weight shift.

Loft on the clubface is crucial for all Weedon's Way players. We are not interested in a square, open or closed clubface at the top of the backswing; rather we are interested in loft on the clubface so that we can access gravity and hit the ball with maximum mass. Loft is attained with the grooves of the club pointing towards the sky. This skyward orientation will guarantee maximum height on the ball flight, which is trajectory equal to the respective degrees of loft on the particular club.

This clubface position brings the whole club in line with the body so it can access gravity and master a pivot that is as close as possible to a 100 per cent rotation. This will create a small moment of inertia and provide the necessary mass to hit the ball.

These two changes to this player's swing will catapult their handicap to a lower number, if learnt well.

c. Low handicapper

A golfer with a low handicap needs to learn three main skills to propel them to golf that they never dreamed of. Along with the injury reduction aspect of Weedon's Way, the following three skills are essential to quality ball striking.

The first would be to introduce the player to the ground, to drive the swing. As we have said before, the flexing and extending of the legs at the knees creates the rotation that keeps the body over the ball and prevents drifting. During the pivot, the feet push down hard on the turf, allowing the hips to swivel or turn around the fixed access of the spine. The ground pushes upwards, friction keeping the feet in place, the head over the ball and the torso centred between the feet. The result of these powerful opposing forces is the formation of a rock-solid platform to power the swing's pivot.

The core of the body, which controls this pivot, harnesses the power of the body's mass as it turns around the spine. The magnitude of this power is raised by increasing the downward pressure of the feet and gravity because, as Newton's third law predicts, it produces an equal force that pushes upwards. The significant force needed to rotate the body's core is greatly assisted by this powered base. The rotation of the body mass takes place on the body's transverse plane, which dissects the body along a plane that is perpendicular to the angle of the spine. This kinetic sequence requires dynamic balance to prevent any lateral leakage. To put this into layman's language, the down-and-up weight shift against the ground, which is a vertical force, creates pure rotation! Telling the learner to rotate will create lateral movement. This vertical force will create massive power.

The second skill is to put loft on the clubface. As for the player with a higher handicap, the grooves of the clubface point skywards. This skyward clubface position will guarantee maximum height of the ball flight and prodigious distance along with the ground forces applied.

Once the elite player has tapped into the vertical forces and loft has been accessed, the last skill to be learnt is to make the golfer's moment of inertia small. This will be done by keeping the left arm under the right shoulder, enabling the sweet spot of the clubface to be closer to the body's centre of rotation, the spine. The moment of inertia is a measure of the opposition that a body (the clubhead) exhibits to its speed around an axis, which may or may not be fixed. The left arm under the right shoulder makes the distance from the body's rotational centre shorter, which allows the body to move faster and to deliver all the energy created and stored into the ball. This in turn will fly the ball to the target.

So to recap: three essential skills must be learnt by a player with a low handicap to take them into the professional ranks:

- Down-and-up weight shift;
- Loft on the clubface;
- Left arm under the right shoulder.

d. Scratch player

The scratch player, along with the player with a low handicap, must learn the three skills:

- Down-and-up weight shift;
- Loft on the clubface;
- Left arm under the right shoulder.

To reach a professional standard, these skills must be mastered. In addition, the player must be taught grip pressures, swing tempos and an understanding of how gravity can add power to the swing.

e. Player with disabilities

It is important for the professional coach to gain some basic knowledge about the learner's disability during the introduction to the lesson. Enquire about any physical, psychological or medical limitations. It is also important to find out the learner's motive for taking instruction. If they have been sent by a doctor or therapist, there might not be much fun in the lesson as the pupil might see it as rehabilitation rather than sport. If this is the case, finding a physically challenged partner to learn with might be helpful. While all individuals must provide their own motivation, an enthusiastic, supportive, patient and persevering coach means so much to a disadvantaged player who may be struggling to muster enthusiasm.

When teaching Weedon's Way to a disabled learner, progress will be made by use of tools of learning which hopefully will encourage the player to enjoy golf again, so that they will look forward once more to playing a round. With all disabilities, improvement in the player's ball flight will push them to a credible level of competence. We are also confident that a good standard of rehabilitation will take place during the teaching sessions.

Chapter 10

More advanced analysis

a. Relevant physics
   1. Newton's three laws
   2. Pushing mass into the ground creates momentum
b. Basics of Weedon's Way
   1. Loft
   2. No axis tilt
   3. Where is "behind the ball?"
   4. Resist the throw-out
   5. Smaller moment of inertia creates bigger mass to hit with
c. Research
   1. Purpose
   2. Methods
   3. Results
   4. Conclusions
d. Unknowns that need to be investigated

a. Relevant physics

1. Newton's three laws

For a long time now, golf coaches have had the task of teaching swings to their students. Like all fashions, new methods spring up every year. Like clockwork, the old methods vanish and new ones appear. This is an ongoing problem for the jobbing golf coach. There are so many different ideas, and the continual changes create problems for credible information.

But let's get out of teaching fads and delve into the real substance – physics! This is obviously the tool that drives every machine – even the golf swing. Let us introduce every golfer to the genius of Sir Isaac Newton, the greatest golf coach of them all!

Newton was a physicist whose laws of classical mechanics first explained motion in the seventeenth century. We believe his three laws of force and motion should be in the toolbox of every sports coach! If there is no understanding of these laws, we believe golf, and sport in general, cannot be taught correctly.

The power creates the shape of the swing. Newton's three laws—(1) inertia; (2) acceleration; and (3) action–reaction—provide coaches with a solid understanding of mechanical cause and effect in the swing. Force creates motion.

2. Pushing mass into the ground creates momentum

As discussed earlier, Newton's third law says that for every action force there is a reaction force, equal in size and opposite in direction. Forces always come in pairs, known as action–reaction pairs. Describing action–reaction force pairs is a simple matter of identifying the *two* interacting objects and making two statements describing who is *pushing* on whom and in what *direction*. The flexing and extending of the legs at the knees creates the rotation of the body.

This pushing against the ground and pushing up feels as if you are going down and up. This is called "vertical force". This vertical force creates pure rotation above the knees. It's a paradox: the more you push down into the ground, the more you can push up. Pushing your mass into the ground through your legs creates the Big Mo!

b. Basics of Weedon's Way

1. *Loft*

At the top of the backswing, the grooves of the clubface will point towards the sky. Golfers should not care whether their clubface is square, closed or open. They should just care that there is loft on the face. This will allow gravity to access the club and drop it into the impact zone. This clubface position will guarantee maximum height on your ball flight, that is a trajectory equal to the respective degrees of loft of the particular iron or wood. With this clubface position, it is difficult to hook the ball now there is no axis tilt in the swing.

2. *No axis tilt*

In Weedon's Way we have taken out the axis tilt, which is vital to the classic upper body swing. This sliding of the hips at the start of the downswing sets off the kinetic chain and begins the shallowing of the shaft and regaining of the loft on the clubface. It also enables the upper body swinger to make contact with the ground pre-impact, to power the body. In theory, the weight of the upper body swinger goes up on the backswing, down on the downswing and then pushes up again pre-impact.

Weedon's Way has no axis tilt. The body weight goes down into the ground when the club goes up and around. This is where the kinetic chain starts. Then, when the club comes down, the weight is pushed up off the ground. Gravity can now access the club and drop it into the impact zone. The Weedon's Way player has no reason to retain loft on the face as it never left it, and has no need for the club to be shallowed out.

The axis tilt puts too much torque on the spine and is a great cause of injury in golf. As we mentioned before, we believe that putting the axis tilt in a golf swing is like giving arsenic for a bellyache!

3. Where is "behind the ball"?

Behind the ball is behind your head. When the arms have the same characteristics as the transverse body pivot, the right side of your body, hips and shoulders go behind you. The coach should say something along the lines of, "Get your right side behind the ball, not your body!" If you were to get your body behind the ball, your body would have to move laterally and contain an axis tilt. The body should pivot rotationally, not laterally.

4. Resist the throw-out

If you use the ground on the backswing and the arms have the same characteristics as the body, then gravity can access the club. When you push up on the ground, the club drops towards the impact zone. Remember, the arms are heavy and loose. What is heavy going up is light coming down. This prevents throw-out.

5. *Smaller moment of inertia creates bigger mass to hit with*

Because the arms are dead and have the body's characteristics on the takeaway, they stay on the same tilt as they started. This enables the club and its sweet spot to stay closer to the body's rotation, creating more depth in the golf swing and small moments of inertia. On the downswing with loft on the clubface and the shaft under the right shoulder, gravity can access the club, which resists throw-out and keeps the moment of inertia smaller. This enables the player to use more mass to hit the ball, and the body will stall less at impact as power is being released through the arms to the clubface to propel the ball.

This takes us on to COAM. Weedon's Way harnesses one of the laws governing physical matter. This is called conservation of angular momentum (COAM). Physics tells us that when an object rotates around a fixed axis, it rotates at a constant speed provided the object stays at the same distance from the axis. If the object is brought closer to the axis, it automatically speeds up. Likewise, if it is moved further away from the axis, it slows down. So a small moment of inertia adheres to the law of COAM.

c. **Research**

EMG research has demonstrated that Weedon's Way uses different muscles than the conventional swing,[4] but we wanted to know how this swing produces clubhead speed.

---

[4] American College of Sports Medicine, 2014.

1. Purpose

To determine how Weedon's Way produces clubhead speed.

2. Methods

We used multi-mode, dynamic measurements, video recordings, force plates, an accelerometer, a goniometer and a radar swing speed device for 22 male golfers between the ages of 18 and 72.

3. Results

Three variables were highly correlated to swing speed: vertical force on the ground under the left foot (scratch $r=0.80$, handicap $r=0.61$); total Newtons of force during the downswing (scratch $r=0.80$, handicap $r=0.61$); and vertical acceleration of the body (scratch $r=0.79$, handicap $r=0.75$). Other measured variables, including total degrees of knee flexion, knee flexing time and horizontal rotation, were not highly correlated to swing speed.

Comparing the tracings of vertical force to the video demonstrated that the force began at the transition and continued past impact, which occurred soon after the initiation. This data means that the vertical force generates an inertial impulse, rather than being summed cumulatively. We verified this by having golfers use minimum knee flexion while still pushing down hard.

The accelerometer tracings show that vertical acceleration of the body from the inertial impulse is translated into horizontal acceleration (rotation) of the body. It also causes the body to accelerate onto the left leg.

The average left knee flexion of all golfers was 30 degrees to a final leg angle of 122 degrees.

4. *Conclusions*

The transverse pivot of Weedon's Way generates an inertial impulse. The inertial impulse generates the sequence of body movements called the "kinetic chain", including rotation and movement onto the left side. These movements create clubhead speed on the downswing.

The optimum angle for left knee flexion is 120 degrees, which, we discovered, is the same as in climbing stairs, jumping and other sports. We determined that scratch golfers make better use of ground forces than handicap golfers.

Weedon's Way differs from the conventional swing in creating no torque between hips and shoulders. It requires no lateral axis tilt and no lifting of the club above the right shoulder. Therefore Weedon's Way is protective of the lower back, shoulders, elbows and wrists.

As we age, our handicaps go up (we assigned 30 handicaps to beginners):

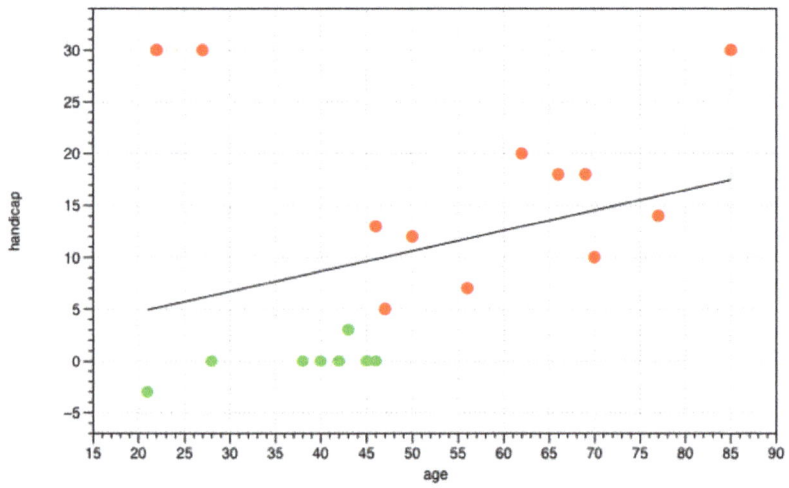

Graph 1

and our swing speeds go down:

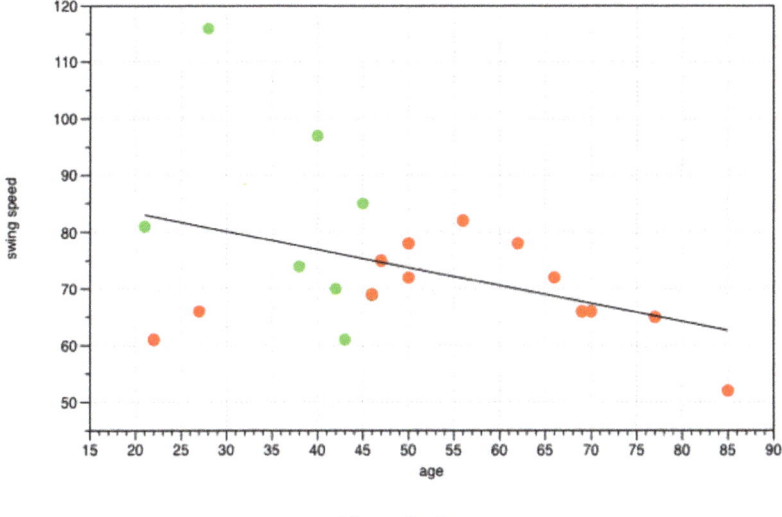

Graph 2

So it isn't surprising that the time it takes to flex and extend our left knee goes up:

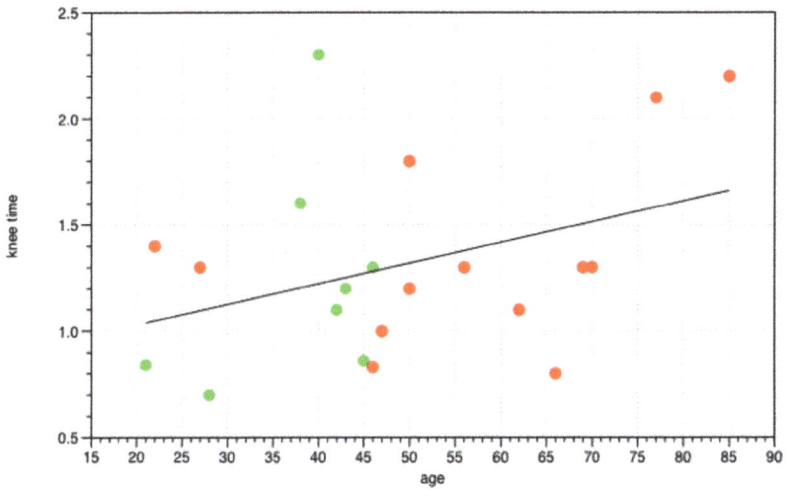

Graph 3

and the total force we produce under our left foot goes down.

Despite ageing, older golfers can flex the left knee just as much as younger golfers can:

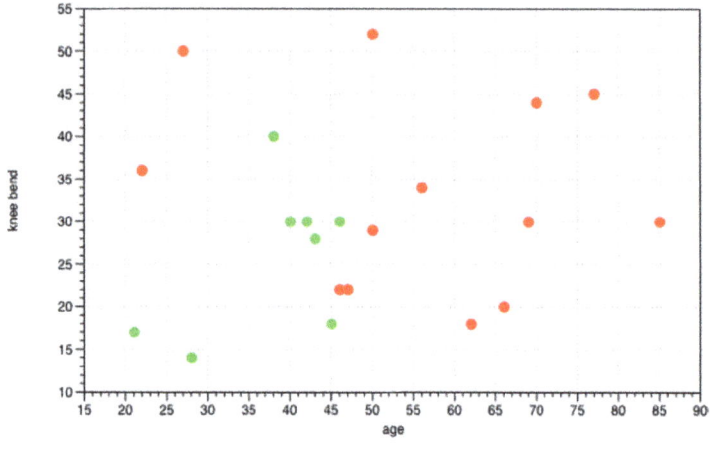

Graph 4

and as a consequence they can produce force over weight on one foot just as well as younger golfers:

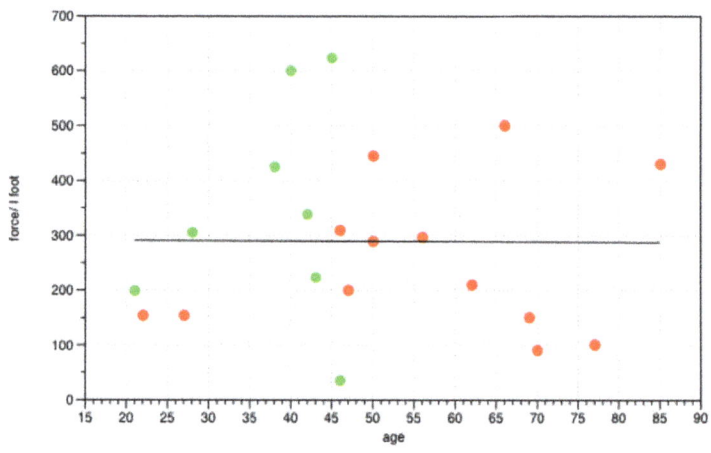

Graph 5

which means their vertical acceleration is even better than younger golfers:

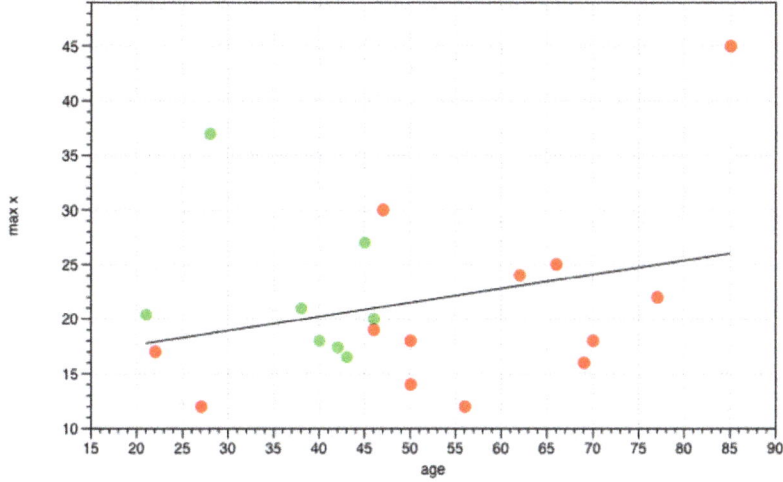

Graph 6

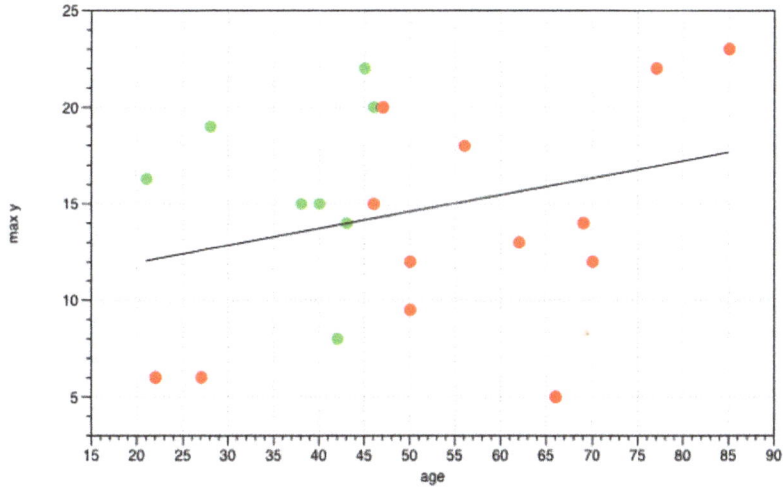

Graph 7

For the following set we asked the question, "Which variables we measured and calculated contribute most to swing speed?" We did this even though swing speed is probably only an approximate, and incomplete, measure of swing quality. But it is a measure we can use for our discussions while understanding that it is a limited criterion.

Many variables turn out to offer little correlation to swing speed. (In the following graphs, assume the steepness of the fit line to mean correlation significance.) For example, swing speed appears to slow down only slightly as knee time increases:

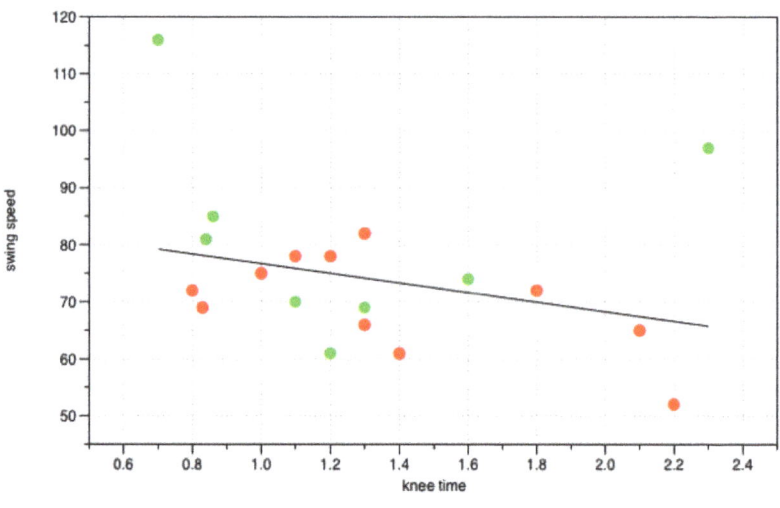

Graph 8

And the force produced by the left foot, minus body weight on one foot, also appears to only slightly increase swing speed:

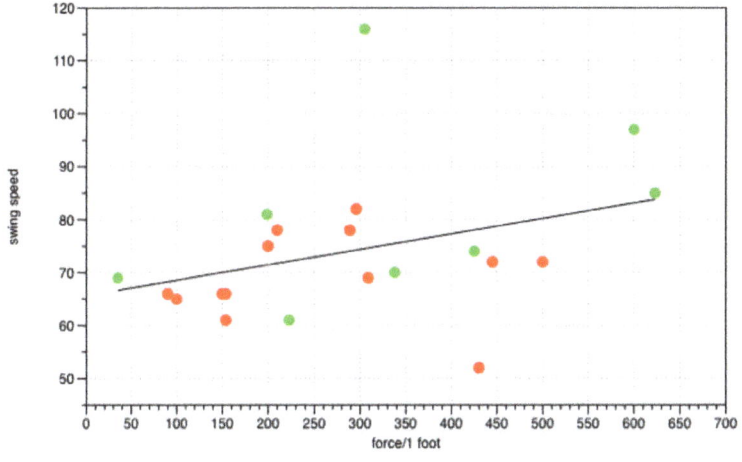

Graph 9

So we should not be surprised that vertical acceleration has a small effect on swing speed:

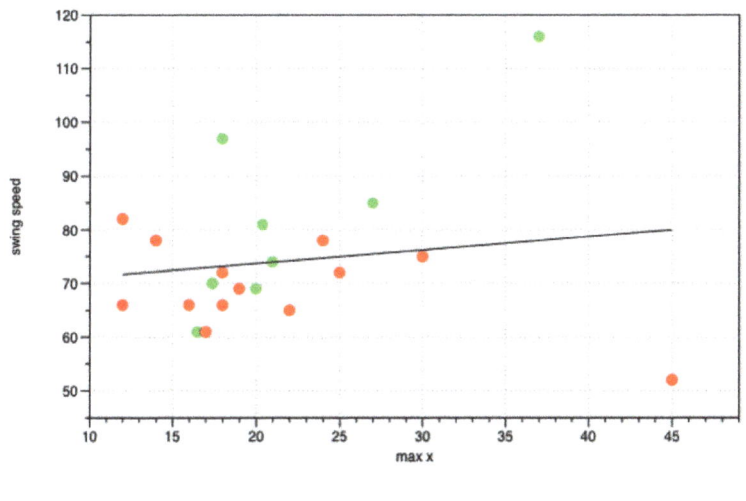

Graph 10

and that horizontal acceleration also has a small effect on swing speed:

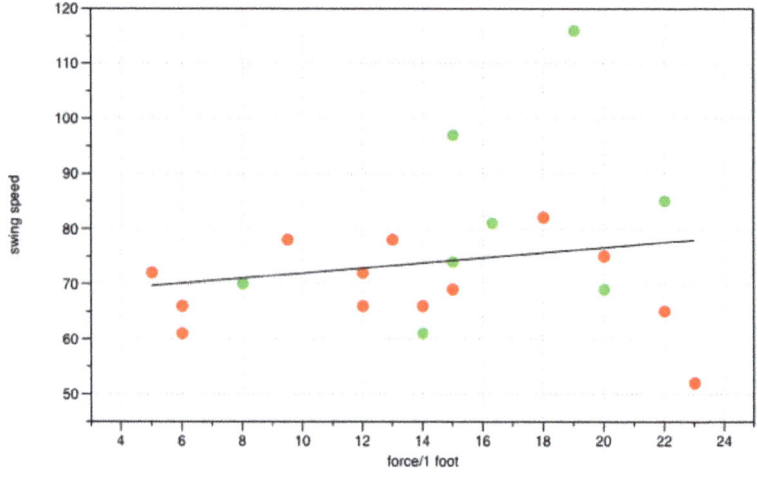

Graph 11

So does any parameter affect swing speed significantly? Yes, there are two – knee angle:

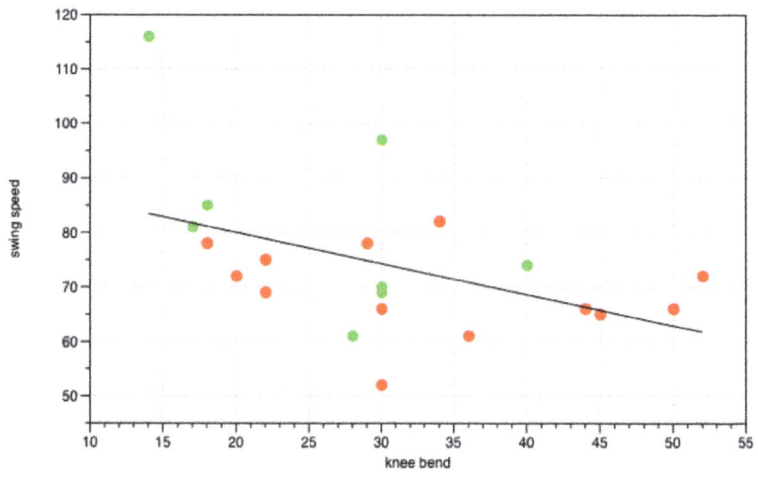

Graph 12

and total force under left foot:

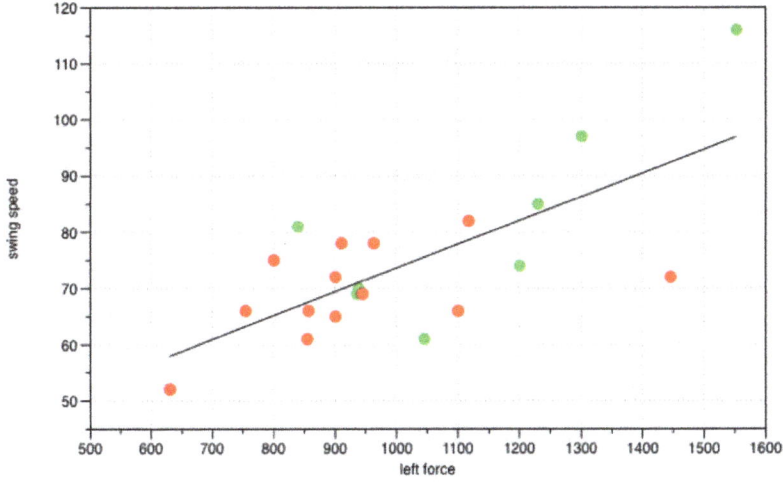

Graph 13

This requires some exploration. Graph 12 says that *less* knee flexion is correlated to more swing speed. This result could be understood as a skew in the data produced by a few subjects who have high swing speeds but small knee bends. Or it could be understood to be saying that the actual amount of knee bend is less important than something else (graph 13). We are impressed by the cluster of green dots around 30 degrees. This suggests that around 30 degrees is an optimum that better players find. Graph 12 strongly suggests that knee bends of greater and less than 30 degrees are sub-optimum.

However, graph 13 has an even steeper slope (rise/run) that says that the most important variable is total force produced. We interpret these two graphs together to be in support of the hypothesis that what matters most in generating swing speeds is the inertial impulse that is generated by an extending knee pushing on the ground.

It will take work on the range to find out what knee angle generates the greatest inertial impulse. Put simply, this analysis suggests that pushing harder is more important than flexing more.

Graph 14 suggests that the subject started with a flexed knee (130 degrees), extended it (to 160 degrees) and then rapidly flexed it (to 90 degrees) The little wobble on the way down in the bend is interesting because it exactly coincides with the peak in force. It may have to do with the club swinging by, and it may have to do with the foot rolling over.

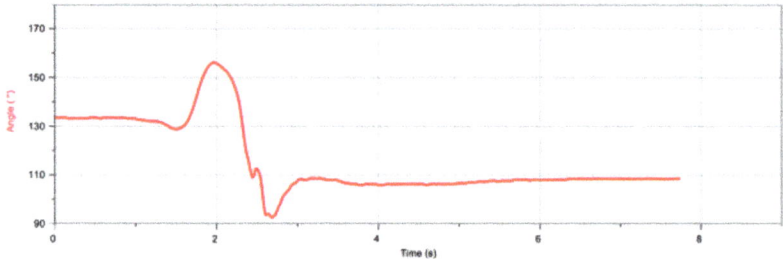

Graph 14

The effect on the force plate was an increase in force as the leg extended (before two seconds) then a return to baseline, then a rapid increase in force (after two seconds). We believe impact occurred exactly at the peak, after two seconds.

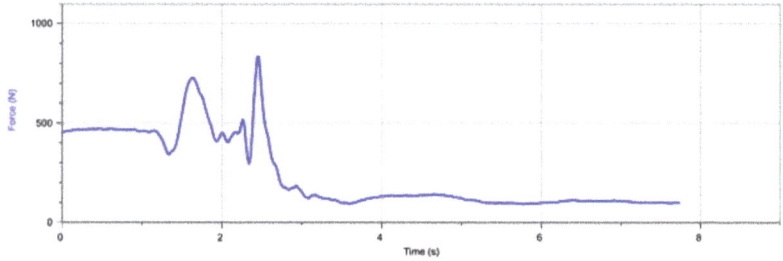

Graph 15

So this means two things: first, the subject does not kink their knee at the top of the backswing. Second, and quite significantly, they create force with the right leg by flexing the knee.

Let us now look at the following force charts. If we add the left and right foot peak forces (939 + 634) we get 1570 newtons. Assuming the force were used to raise the body by one metre (probably too big) in 0.6 seconds (the time of the force generation), this gives a power of 2625 watts (3.5 horsepower).

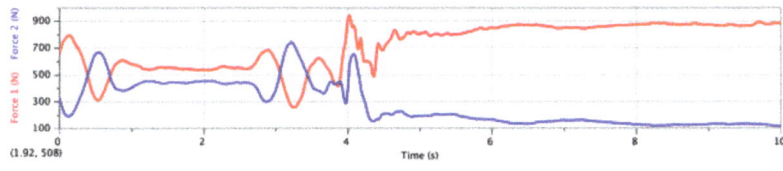

Graph 16

If we take someone who produces the same left foot force and no right force, as in graph 17, we have 934 newtons raising the body by the same one metre (again too big) in 0.6 seconds, which gives a power of 1556 watts (2.1 horsepower). This means that with the same effort, the second subject is only producing 0.6 of the power of the first subject. (It is possible that some of the right foot power that occurs when the second subject shifts their weight from right to left before impact increases their rotation.)

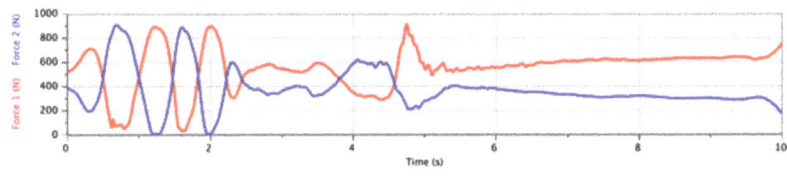

Graph 17

So the conclusion is to use both feet, and to do it quickly.

d. Unknowns that need to be investigated

The lower back is commonly susceptible to injury in the modern golf swing (upper body). During the swing, the hip joints and thoracic spine are limited in their movement so the lumbar spine sacrifices stability to obtain more movement. This irregular movement in the lumbar spine created by the axis tilt can be one of the main causes of injuries in the lower back. Limited spine and hip movement are two common findings in male golfers.

We believe that, owing to the absence of the axis tilt in Weedon's Way, research is needed to show that there would be fewer injuries using this approach than in the classic swing and its rivals.

We believe our approach would be of interest to other parties carrying out research on the lower back.

Chapter 11

How Weedon's Way differs from other approaches

a. Conventional (upper body) swing

b. Stack and tilt

c. Others

Beginners, children and adults of all ages are being taught plane of the golf swing as their introduction to golf. This is like the times tables to maths, and the dictionary to English – an absolute necessity. At the moment there are various approaches to teaching golf: the conventional modern swing, the stack and tilt, one plane and right-sided golf. But nothing is as simple and injury free as Weedon's Way.

I hear you ask, "Why are you so confident that Weedon's Way is understandable and reduces the risk of injury?"

We believe there are three main reasons:

- No axis tilt;
- Transverse pivot;
- Loft on the clubface.

All the other approaches mentioned have a lateral motion on the downswing. This axis tilt is a bending backwards with a bump of the hips towards the target. This motion puts strain on the lower back and can cause lower back injury. This movement is not present in Weedon's Way.

The transverse body pivot eradicates any lateral motion in the golf swing. It is a front-to-back, back-to-front weight shift pushing against the ground to create pure rotation. Any swing, including an axis tilt, must contain a lateral shift.

Also, the other approaches conduct a square (open) and closed clubface at the terminus of the backswing. Weedon's Way doesn't! We are just concerned that there is loft on the clubface. Loft is defined as a "backward slope, measured in degrees of the face of a golf club's head". The term "loft" means that the grooves of the clubface point towards the sky at the top of the backswing.

These three motions are unique to Weedon's Way. It introduces a unique kinaesthetic feel consistently in sync with the laws of physics and mechanics. It is a question of mechanics over opinion.

Chapter 12

Injury prevention—to save your back

a. Backswing

b. Downswing

c. Impact

d. Finish

Response to Sean Foley's upper body swing golf digest article

In 2010, Sean Foley offered four hints to help prevent lower back injury. These were:
- Backswing: to maintain a flexed right knee and to turn the left shoulder downwards.
- Downswing: to use the ground to create the swing. It feels as if the player is preparing to jump up using the thigh muscles and glutes in a squat move.

- Impact: 90 per cent of the body weight should be over the left leg, and the shoulders and hips should be level and turning open.
- Finish: thrust the pelvis towards the target, absorbing the stress with the left glutes and core muscles. Push forward and stand up.[45]

a. Backswing

We believe that the transverse body pivot, front-to-back, back-to-front weight shift will allow the right leg to extend without putting stress on the bottom vertebrae. This pivot means the right side of your body goes behind your head, not to the right of the ball. Any lateral movement to the right of the ball (the upper swing is behind the ball) will create a movement at the start of the downswing which will put torque on the spine. The proposed weight shift will not.

b. Downswing

The lateral squat on the downswing will be followed by an axis tilt which will put pressure on the spine. Our transverse pivot creates a movement down into the ground on the backswing and a push up off the ground on the downswing. This vertical force creates greater rotation than trying to rotate, which we have proved by way of scientific research. Our

---

[5] Sean Foley, 'Four steps to save your back', *Golf Digest,* March 2010. Foley went on to work with Tiger Woods, Justin Rose and many more PGA tour players. He is regarded as one of the best golf coaches in the world. On this article he collaborated with Craig Davies, a chiropractor and fitness trainer.

swing is without any lateral motion and therefore greatly reduces the risk of injury.

c. Impact

At impact, Weedon's Way is not trying to rotate. The player is trying to push up from the ground for both feet. This vertical push will rotate the body. Once again, no lateral motion, and no ouch!

d. Finish

There is no thrusting forward of the pelvis towards the target. Weedon's Way finishes the launch from the ground with a balanced finish, with no arch in the back, and the player's weight is over their left side. Once again there is no lateral motion or axis tilt, and no stress on the spine.

As mentioned earlier, Morowitz says, "The purpose of this book is to discuss and present evidence for the general thesis that the flow of energy through a system acts to organise a system."[6] We believe that we have discovered this in Weedon's Way, and that the pushing against and off the ground recruits the right muscles to coordinate the body's flow of energy to drive the golf swing without injury.

---

[6] Harold J. Morowitz, *Energy Flow in Biology*.

Chapter 13

Research

37th International Society of Biomechanics in Sport Conference, Oxford, OH, United States, July 21-25, 2019

A COMPARISON BETWEEN THE MODERN AND THE LOWER BODY GOLF SWING TECHNIQUES– PILOT STUDY WITH IMPLICATIONS FOR LOWER BACK INJURY RISK

Sarah Breen[1], Katja Osterwald[2], Chris Richter[3], and Erich Petushek[1,4]

School of Health and Human Performance, Northern Michigan University, Marquette, USA[1]
Athlone Institute of Technology, Athlone, Ireland[2]
Department of Sport Medicine, Sport Surgery Clinic, Dublin, Ireland[3]
College of Human Medicine, Michigan State University, East Lansing, USA[4]

The purpose of this study was to compare the biomechanical characteristics of the lower body swing to modern swing techniques, with a focus on lower back injury risk. Fifteen male individuals free from lower back injury participated in this study. Nine participants utilized the modern swing (age = 48.0 ± 13.6 years; height = 176.8 ± 4.4 cm; mass = 82.1 ± 5.3 kg) while six utilized the lower body swing (age = 53.9 ±12.1 years; height = 182.9 ± 6.1 cm; mass = 92.5 ± 14.8 kg). Whole body kinematics were recorded with a ten-camera motion analysis system while individuals performed 5 shots with a driver for maximum distance. Continuous waveform and discrete point analysis was used to explore the differences between these two techniques. The lower body swing demonstrated favourable kinematics in the majority of variables related to lower back pain and lumbar load.

KEYWORDS: kinematics, motion analysis, lumbar, spine, biomechanics

INTRODUCTION: Abnormal swing biomechanics have been highlighted as a major cause of golf injury (Gluck, Bendo & Spivak 2008; Lindsay and Vandervoort, 2014; McHardy, Pollard & Luo 2007). The majority of these injuries occurred at ball impact or follow through of the golf swing (McHardy et al., 2007), likely due to the large forces during these phases (Lim, Chow & Chae 2012). Modifications to swing technique may reduce spinal load/ injury risk, however limited empirical evidence supports this claim (Cole and Grimshaw, 2015).

While the modern swing technique has been developed and adopted for improving performance (e.g., Hume, Keogh & Reid 2005; Myers et al., 2008), these characteristics may also contribute to increased risk for low back injury (i.e., greater X-factor, lateral bend or crunch factor, follow-through hyperextension, forward tilt, etc.). Numerous, theoretical and clinical commentaries have suggested that the classic style swing has advantages over the modern swing due to the potentially decreased spinal motion and loading (Cole and Grimshaw, 2014; Cole and Grimshaw, 2015; Gluck et al., 2008). To date, only one study has compared the classic vs modern swing (Ashish, Shweta & Singh 2008), however, only electromyography (EMG) data of the oblique's and erector spinae was captured. Results revealed greater erector spinae activation in the modern swing with greater oblique activation in the classic swing. This limited evidence and methodological shortcomings (e.g., EMG data only, no performance evaluation, large variability, order effects, iron use, and lack of technical verification/quality) warrants further investigation comparing various swing techniques.

One potential method that could ameliorate spinal loads while maintaining or even improving performance could be to increase lower body motions to produce the necessary rotational characteristics versus the upper body. This 'lower body' style swing has the potential to produce similar spinal loading characteristics to that of the 'classic' style but performance benefits seen from the 'modern' style. The lower body style has been documented in coaching texts (Weedon and Harris, 2015) but has yet to be empirically investigated for its potential protective and performance benefits. Therefore, the purpose of this study was to analyse biomechanical characteristics between two different golf swing techniques - the modern and the lower body swing.

METHODS: Fifteen male golfers free from musculoskeletal injury took part in the study. Ethical approval was granted by the ethics committee of the Leeds Beckett University, and all participants provided informed consent. Participants were divided into a modern (n = 9) and lower body (n = 6) swing group based on their preferred swing technique (see Fig 1).

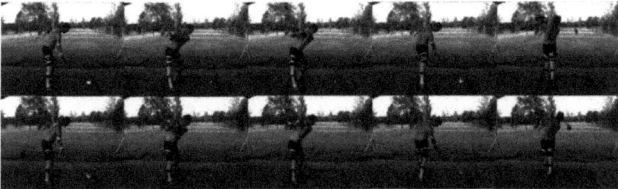

Figure 1: Lower body (top) and modern (bottom) swing techniques.

Participants performed five shots for maximum distance and 3D kinematics were recorded using a ten-camera (Vantage V5, Vicon, UK) motion analysis system (250 Hz). A set of 62 reflective markers (1.4 cm diameter) were attached to the participants using double sided tape, at bony landmarks on the lower limbs, pelvis and trunk per the Vicon Plug-in-Gait markerset, in combination with marker clusters on fore and upper arm as well as the thigh and shank. Vicon Nexus 2.3 was used to analyse the motion data, which was filtered using a fourth-order Butterworth filter (cut-off frequency of 15Hz (Kristianslund, Krosshaug & van den Bogert 2012)). Segment and joint angles were calculated as described in Winter, 2009. The swing movement was time normalized to 303 frames (three phases) and landmark registered to the following key events (address, top of back swing, ball impact and end of follow through) (Ramsey, 2006). Subsequently to the landmark registration, all trials of a subject were averaged to generate a representable mean. The aim of this pilot investigation was to provide initial data for the feasibility of further investigations exploring the benefits of the lower body swing in reducing lower back injuries. Thus, variables of interest were: the thorax (in relation to pelvis and global) angles, angular velocity and angular acceleration as well as the crunch factor (product of trunk abduction angle and trunk rotational velocity). This exploratory analysis utilized continuous waveform analysis of the various kinematic variables and discrete point analysis of potential velocity and acceleration variables that are likely related to lower back pain and joint loading (Grimshaw and Burden, 2000; Lindsay and Horton, 2002; Cole and Grimshaw, 2014). To identify differences in examined kinematic measures between the groups, Cohens *d* effect size was calculated in a point-by-point manner to determine relevance of a difference ($d > 0.5$ = moderate; $d > 0.8$ = large) (Cohen, 1988). However, since the main goal was exploratory in nature and due to the small sample size, statistical analyses should be interpreted with caution. All data processing and statistical analyses were performed using MATLAB (R2015a, MathWorks Inc., USA).

RESULTS: Participants in the lower body swing group were aged 53.9 (±12.1 SD) years old, 182.9 (±6.1 SD) cm tall and 92.5 (±14.8 SD) kg. Participants in the modern swing group aged 48.0 (±13.6 SD), 176.8 (±4.4 SD) cm tall and 82.1 (±5.3 SD) kg. The average handicap for the lower body swing group in this study was 15.8 (±6.3 SD) and for the modern swing group 9.1 (±5.1 SD). On average, the participants in the lower body swing group had been playing golf for 17.6 (±11.9 SD) years, while the participants who performed the modern swing had been playing for 23.4 (±15.3 SD) years. Lower body swing participants averaged 2.3 (±2.7 SD) rounds per week, while the modern swing participants averaged 3.0 (±1.9 SD) rounds per week.

Table 1: Kinematic differences between the lower body and modern swing.

	Lower Body		Modern			
	Mean	SD	Mean	SD	p value	d
Thorax-Pelvis Rotation Velocity (°/sec)	356.19	49.46	436.98	82.33	0.066	1.05
Thorax-Pelvis Rotation Acceleration (°/sec^2)	6253.68	2429.78	9008.15	1514.03	0.040	1.14
Thorax-Pelvis Abduction Velocity (°/sec)	97.48	24.44	155.91	33.79	0.006	1.41
Thorax-Pelvis Abduction Acceleration (°/sec^2)	4347.38	2146.03	5904.96	1096.05	0.144	0.86
Thorax Flexion Velocity (°/sec)	95.41	34.72	131.08	31.11	0.094	0.97

Thorax to pelvis rotation separation angle (X-factor) was substantially lower in the lower body compared to modern swing technique at the top of the backswing and during ball impact (see Fig 3-A). Thorax to pelvis abduction (side bending) angle was lower in the lower body compared to modern swing prior to ball impact (see Fig 3-B). Trunk flexion to pelvis angle was slightly lower in the lower body compared to the modern swing prior to impact (see Fig 3-C). Near ball impact, maximum thorax to pelvis rotational angular velocity and acceleration were lower in the lower body compared to the modern swing (see Table 1). Thorax to pelvis abduction velocity and acceleration were also lower prior to and near ball impact. Maximum thorax to pelvis flexion velocity was substantially lower prior to ball impact in the lower body compared to the modern swing. Finally, the crunch factor appeared to be slightly lower in the lower body compared the modern swing near ball impact (see Fig 3-D).

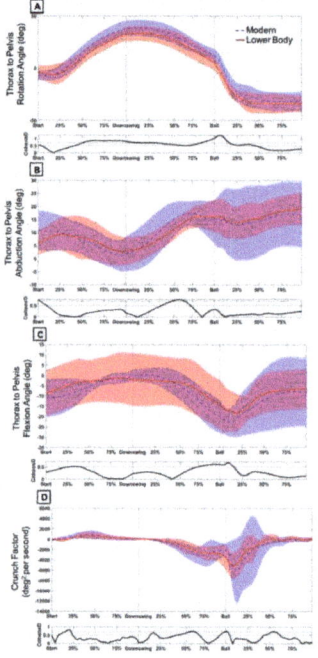

Figure 2: Kinematic difference between the modern and lower body swing techniques.

DISCUSSION: Large differences were found in the thorax to pelvis separation angle (X-factor) between the two groups at the top of the backswing and at impact. These findings suggest that during the lower body swing, the rotational and compressive load acting on the spine may be reduced at these time points (Cole and Grimshaw, 2014). Decreasing hip/shoulder separation angle has also been shown to be a positive adaptation following a coaching intervention with an individual with low back pain (Grimshaw and Burden, 2000), as well as following a shortened back swing (Bulbulian, Ball & Seaman 2001). In addition, differences in spinal rotation have been found between individuals with and without low back pain (Lindsay and Horton, 2002). While it is clear that other spinal motions besides rotation occur during a golf swing, aggressive axial twisting has been identified as a significant risk factor for LBP (Lindsay and Vandervoort, 2014). On the contrary, increased torso – pelvis separation angle and rotational velocity has been shown to be related to improved golf performance (Myers et al., 2008). Thus, there seems to be a performance-injury risk trade off that may influence an individual's desire to modify their swing technique (Cole and Grimshaw, 2015), if the notion that this increased stretch is contributing to injury risk. However, it is unlikely that the stretch (e.g., during the backswing), is contributing to excessive spinal loads as the downswing and impact phase is likely the phases in which most stress and injuries occur (Cole and Grimshaw, 2014; Hosea, 1990; Lim et al., 2012).

CONCLUSION: While very few studies have compared various swing techniques or modifications thereof, abnormal swing biomechanics have been highlighted as a major cause of injury. The current pilot investigation provides preliminary data for the feasibility of further research investigating the lower body swing and its potential to reduce lower back injury risk. The kinematic characteristics of the lower body swing has the potential to reduce lower back loading, however further higher-powered, prospective or longitudinal studies should be conducted to evaluate the benefits of this novel technique.

REFERENCES
Ashish, A., Shweta, S., and Singh, S.J. (2008) Comparison of lumbar and abdominal muscle activation during two types of golf swing: An EMG analysis. *International Journal of Sports Science* 12(4), 59-71.
Bulbulian, R., Ball, K. A., & Seaman, D. R. (2001). The short golf backswing: effects on performance and spinal health implications. *Journal of Manipulative & Physiological Therapeutics*, 24(9), 569-575.
Cohen, J. (1988). Statistical power analysis for the behavioural sciences (2nd ed.). Hillsdale, NJ: Lawrence Earlbaum Associates.
Cole, M. and Grimshaw, P. (2014). The crunch factor's role in golf-related low back pain. *The Spine Journal* 14(5), 799–807.
Cole, M. and Grimshaw, P. (2015) The biomechanics of the modern golf swing: Implications for lower back injuries. *Sports Medicine* 46(3), 339–351.
Gluck, G., Bendo, J., and Spivak, J. (2008) The lumbar spine and low back pain in golf: a literature review of swing biomechanics and injury prevention. *The Spine Journal* 8(5), 778–788.
Grimshaw, P. N., & Burden, A. M. (2000). Case report: reduction of low back pain in a professional golfer. *Medicine and Science in Sports and Exercise* 32(10), 1667-1673.
Hosea, T. (1990) Biomechanical analysis of the golfer's back. *Science and Golf*, 43-48.
Hume, P. A., Keogh, J., & Reid, D. (2005). The role of biomechanics in maximising distance and accuracy of golf shots. *Sports Medicine*, 35(5), 429-449.
Kristianslund E., Krosshaug T., van den Bogert A.J. (2012) Effect of low pass filtering on joint moments from inverse dynamics: implications for injury prevention. *Journal of Biomechanics* 45, 666-671.
Lim, Y., Chow, J., and Chae, W. (2012). Lumbar spinal loads and muscle activity during a golf swing. *Sports Biomechanics* 11(2), 197–211.
Lindsay, D. and Horton, J. (2002) Comparison of spine motion in elite golfers with and without low back pain. *Journal of Sports Sciences* 20(8), 599–605.
Lindsay, D. and Vandervoort, A. (2014) Golf-related low back pain: A review of causative factors and prevention strategies. *Asian Journal of Sports Medicine* 5(4). E24289
McHardy, A., Pollard, H., and Luo, K. (2007) One-Year Follow-up Study on Golf Injuries in Australian Amateur Golfers. *The American Journal of Sports Medicine* 35(8), 1354–1360.
Myers, J., Lephart, S., Tsai, Y., Sell, T., Smoliga, J., and Jolly, J. (2008) The role of upper torso and pelvis rotation in driving performance during the golf swing. *Journal of Sports Sciences* 26(2), 181–188.
Ramsey, J.O. (2006) *Functional Data Analysis*. John Wiley and Sons.
Weedon, R. and Harris, J. (2015) *The lower body golf swing*. Grosvenor House Publishing.

ACKNOWLEDGEMENTS: We would like to thank Vicon Motion Systems Ltd UK for their use of equipment and technical assistance during data collection.

www.ingramcontent.com/pod-product-compliance
Lightning Source LLC
LaVergne TN
LVHW070013090426
835508LV00048B/3385